FIREPLACE STOVES, HEARTHS, & INSERTS

". . . containing every useful invention known to stove manufacturers."
SEARS, ROEBUCK AND CO. CATALOGUE, *1897*

FIREPLACE STOVES, HEARTHS, & INSERTS

A Coal- & Wood-Burner's Guide & Catalog

Geri Harrington

HARPER & ROW, PUBLISHERS, NEW YORK
Cambridge, Hagerstown, Philadelphia, San Francisco,
London, Mexico City, São Paulo, Sydney

1817

By the same author

THE COLLEGE COOKBOOK
SUMMER GARDEN WINTER KITCHEN
THE SALAD BOOK
THE WOOD-BURNING STOVE BOOK
GROW YOUR OWN CHINESE VEGETABLES
NEVER TOO OLD

FIRST EDITION

Designed by Sheila Lynch

LIBRARY OF CONGRESS CATALOG CARD NUMBER: 80-7587

ISBN: 0-06-011821-0
       0-06-090804-1 pbk.

80 81 82 83 10 9 8 7 6 5 4 3 2 1

Contents

Part Four: THE WOOD- AND COAL-BURNER'S CATALOG

Introduction:
A Realistic Look at
Our Energy Options

Now that everyone agrees there is an energy crisis, the consumer is snowed under with suggestions for solving it. Consumer magazines, trade journals, television programs, forums, and seminars all promote one or another point of view. Without the facts—and they are not easy to come by—it is hard for the consumer to distinguish between the patent-medicine panacea and the real cure.

Each energy source has its spokesman; the architects opt for solar heat; the oil companies say oil conservation is the answer; the utilities insist nuclear power is inevitable—with coal as a temporary solution until nuclear capability can be developed more fully. Only the consumer is strongly sold on wood. Who is right? Let's look at a few facts.

Solar Energy

In 1944, in Lexington, Massachusetts, MIT scientists constructed one of the first homes heated entirely by solar energy. After studying its operation through several New England winters, they concluded that the system worked, but at a price beyond the purse of the average consumer. As the MIT report put it, the system is "technically acceptable . . . [but] the limitations are primarily economic." More than thirty-five years later, the same situation prevails. In 1979, a report by Los Alamos, done for the Department of Energy, concluded: "Solar residential space heating costs remain higher than conventional natural gas and heating oil prices." And that same year, the New England Energy Congress, in "Prospects for Solar Energy," said: ". . . solar heat is approximately three times as expensive . . . and it is not expected that the collection efficiency of solar systems will be tripled within the next decade."

One of the difficulties in lowering the costs of solar installations is that plastics form a large part of the necessary equipment. Since most of these plastics are made from oil derivatives, their costs go up along with the rise in the price of oil. This Catch-22 situation may be partially resolved when coal derivatives are substituted (as they are technically capable of being), but this, of course, depends on the revitalization of the coal industry.

Another problem is that existing houses are not easily adapted to utilization of solar energy. To heat a typical existing Cape-style house, built to cold-climate specifications—as in Rhode Island, for example—would require about 1,700 square feet of collector installed at a 50–90-degree angle. Since the average Cape would have only about 700 feet of roof, plus possibly another 75–100 square feet of southern window exposure, plus—optimistically—another 100 square feet of usable vertical surface, it would obviously be impossible to find the 1,700-square-foot area required. And we have not even considered the aesthetics of a house gleaming with solar panels over every inch of its southern exposure.

In addition, a 2,000–3,000-gallon water tank would be required to store the heat collected. Many houses do not even have enough land on which to place such a tank. For the system to work at top efficiency, studs of 2 inches by 6 inches, rather than the standard 2 by 4's, should have been installed to accommodate the recommended amount of insulation required. Obviously, only new houses, specially designed and built, can even begin to consider solar heat, and their cost must necessarily be far higher than the design and construction of the present standard dwelling. The New England Energy Congress reluctantly concluded: ". . . it is physically impossible to retrofit New England's housing stock with 100% solar heat and hot water." And what is true of New England is equally true of many other parts of the country. While the demands made on solar heating and the longer periods of sunshine that exist in the so-called sun belt are considerably less than in Oregon or Minnesota, for example, winters, even in parts of sunny New Mexico, can be bitter, and the design and construction of the existing houses there are no better suited to retrofitting solar panels than is a Rhode Island Cape.

Much time and money is being spent on the development of solar heating capability but, as one estimate puts it: "The combination of falling solar costs and rising conventional costs should actually make solar [only] *competitive* with oil and gas by the mid-1990's." Since the same estimate also cautions that, unfortunately, "falling solar costs" may not occur, we had better not count on being bailed out by solar energy for some time to come.

Oil

There is certainly no need to comment on the oil situation. Everyone who drives a car, heats a home with oil or electricity (made with oil), works in an office building, or rents an apartment with an oil furnace or boiler in the basement—in other words, just about every American—finds his or her life affected by the incredible and ever-increasing cost of this fossil fuel. Oil cannot solve the energy crisis; oil *is* the energy crisis.

The oil companies, understandably reluctant to see their "black gold" replaced by other fuels, keep stressing conservation and more conservation.

That reminds me of the nineteenth-century story about the small dairy farmer who found his profits eroded by the high cost of winter fodder. He figured if he could get his cows to eat less, he would make more money. So he gradually cut down the amount of fodder.

Every day the cows ate less and his profits rose. When the cows got a little weak on the meager diet, he constructed harnesses to put under their bellies to keep them on their feet. Unfortunately, he never found out if his theory was sound. Just as he was about to realize windfall profits, the darned critters up and died on him.

Happily, the American consumers aren't cows. We can fight back; we can find a better way.

Coal

The extent of our coal deposits makes coal a particularly attractive alternative to oil. The two problems that presently exist, where coal is concerned, are availability and pollution. Availability can be solved easily once the demand for it is certain—and there are already parts of the country where domestic use of wood is rapidly being replaced by the more compact coal.

Pollution is discussed in detail in Chapter 8: What About Pollution? and is not an insurmountable obstacle.

Wood

Because it is a renewable and nonpolluting fuel, wood is the best source of energy we have—and we have a great deal of it. Furthermore, we have it immediately available; it does not have to be mined; the work involved in cutting up trees or deadwood is minor compared to the labor required to bring coal from beneath the earth to the market. As with coal, however, there is no existing network for the transportation of wood from the areas where it is plentiful to the areas where it is scarce. Fortunately, many of the areas where it is plentiful—such as New England—are also the very places that have a dependence on foreign oil that is greater than the national average, and have the longest and bitterest winters. With over 80 percent of the region forested —largely neglected forest, which can, however, be made much more productive in the future—there is estimated to be at minimum a twenty-five-year supply of wood for replacement of other fuels. In the Northwest, factories in Oregon and Washington are already using wood chips and sawdust as their sole fuel, as are some factories in the South. In Vermont and New Hampshire, public utilities are rapidly converting to wood fuel, and in many cases, whole towns are heating with, and getting their electricity from, wood alone. The feasibility of wood heat has been clearly demonstrated to the satisfaction of all but the most obdurate. Many feel that its use would be even more widespread if its production were controlled by such giants as the oil industry, so that its sale would reap high profits. Let us hope this will never happen and let us, as consumers, keep a sharp eye to make sure that it doesn't. The small profiteer in wood is still affected by local conditions and local public opinion; the impersonal operations of large companies are indifferent to these considerations.

In Summary

We need not be dependent on foreign oil; our own oil resources, if made 100 percent available to the United States and not sold abroad, plus the resurgence of the coal industry in the foreseeable future, plus the immediate use of wood as an energy source, form a three-way solution that can take us comfortably through the next several hundred years. During that breathing space, it is quite possible that we will develop a solar technology within the reach of the average homeowner.

If, instead, energy is made a luxury because of excessive profit-taking; if we continue to be dependent on foreign oil because it benefits domestic oil companies; if America's access to its own natural resources is resisted because there is more money to be made in foreign markets; if future energy sources are dominated by the same few companies that control oil, we have only ourselves to blame. It may be time for American citizens and taxpayers to decide that their country's natural resources belong to them, and that the luck and timing that concentrated control of these resources in the hands of a few at the expense of the many can no longer be tolerated. The oil situation is no longer an example of American free enterprise; it is an example of greed and avarice which has turned the making of money into a game programmed so that the consumer always loses.

Let's not be losers any longer. Let's switch to coal and wood wherever practical, with antipollution legislation and government control over the ownership of these natural resources. Oil companies already have a large financial interest in our coal; let us take steps now to make sure it doesn't go the way of oil. And let's keep wood a cottage industry.

"This engraving is from another of the admirably constructed and beautifully designed Stoves, manufactured by Messrs. Gray and Son, of Edinburgh, by Messrs. Hoole & Robson of Sheffield, the whole works have been objects of very general admiration—and of great attraction to all who desire to combine elegance with comfort 'at home.'"
FROM THE ART JOURNAL CATALOGUE AT THE CRYSTAL PALACE EXHIBITION, LONDON *1851*

FIREPLACE STOVES, HEARTHS, & INSERTS

Some Hard Facts About Fireplaces

An open fire in the fireplace is pretty and fun and a luxury that we really can no longer afford. It wastes more heat than it produces; at best, a fireplace is 10 percent efficient. It burns so much wood that in Ben Franklin's day there was a shortage of firewood in and around Philadelphia, due to the excessive use of wood in the large, hopelessly inefficient colonial fireplaces.

In a house with central heating, an open fire in the fireplace increases your heating bill because it uses already warmed room air for combustion. If you have a really efficiently drawing fireplace and chimney, the amount of air taken out of the room can create chilly drafts, trigger the thermostat more often, and make the house thoroughly uncomfortable. At night, when the fire dies down, warm air is eventually drawn up the flue and you awaken to hear the furnace working overtime.

The inefficiency of open fires is not a new discovery. Man has been trying to make fireplaces more efficient ever since he moved his fire from outside to inside his cave. Castles—impossibly difficult structures to heat—finally created real fireplaces by moving the fire from the center of the room to a side wall, with a chimney funneling the smoke and volatiles up through the roof. It took time—until the eighteenth century, to be exact—before mankind developed the principles of sound fireplace design. At that time, an American royalist named Count Rumford studied the fireplace in a scientific manner and came up with a set of principles that would ensure a properly working fireplace. No one ever improved on the count's principles and all good architects have used them to this day. As long as a fireplace is constructed to his specifications, it will work as well as can be expected. To be sure, that's not all that well, but it's better than nothing.

Radiant Heat

One of the reasons a fireplace isn't an efficient heating device is that it produces primarily radiant heat. Radiant heat heats objects, not air. If you stand in front of a fireplace in an icy-cold room, you can roast your front and freeze your back. So aside from the fact that most of the heat produced is lost up the chimney, the little that comes into the room doesn't go very far. The effective range of a fireplace fire can be determined easily—just stand in front of it and back away until the side facing the fire begins to feel chilly. You'll find you don't have to back off very far.

Convective Heat

Convective heat heats the air, not objects. Baseboard heating is convective heat. So is forced hot air. So is solar heat.

The closest a fireplace fire comes to producing convective heat is in the heat given off by the firebrick walls of the firebox. Fireplace users learned early that this kind of heat was desirable, and the fireback was developed to produce more of it. This metal plate covered the back of the firebox and reflected heat into the room. You can buy modern firebacks that perform the same function, but they won't turn your fireplace into a wood stove.

Franklin and the Invention of Convective Heat

Franklin was a stubborn man. He knew that the stoves of the Dutch and German colonists created warm, cozy houses and used comparatively little fuel, but he didn't like them because they hid his view of the fire. Along with most American colonists, he preferred to freeze and watch the dancing flames. When a wood shortage hit Philadelphia, however, he faced up to the fact that something had to be done, so he went to work and produced the "New-Invented Pennsylvanian Fireplace."

Very few people appreciate the sophistication of Franklin's invention, nor is he given credit for the most unusual features of it. What we call "Franklin fireplaces" today would irritate him no end; he would never have settled for an enclosed firebox with an optional view of the open fire.

What the original Franklin fireplace did that was so revolutionary was to use *outside air for both combustion and convection.* His stove required a ducting channel to the outdoors. The ducting channel led in air to both the firebox, to feed oxygen to the fire, and to a convection chamber constructed in the back of the firebox. The air in the convection chamber was heated by the fire in the firebox but was sealed off from it so that no smoke leaked through. This heated air flowed into the room from outlets on either side. It worked on the principle of convection, by means of which heated air rises. As the cold outside air was heated, therefore, it automatically rose to the vents and out into room, making space for more cold air to enter. Natural convection kept this process producing warm air as long as there was a fire in the firebox.

Because of the use of outside air for combustion, a minimum amount of air was drawn from the room and chilly drafts were minimized. In addition, Franklin designed his "Fireplace" with a shield that could be put in place for the night or whenever the fire was meant to go out. This further prevented loss of warm room air as the fire was dying down and was considerably superior to our modern practice of putting a screen in front of the fire and going to bed with the flue damper open because we are too tired to stay up and wait for the fire to go out—at which point, we could close the damper.

Incidentally, illustrations never indicate that Franklin meant his fires to be built not directly on the "Fireplace" floor but in a grate, a more efficient method.

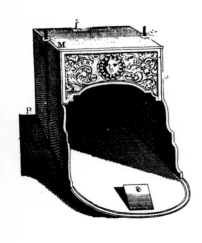

*Ben Franklin's
"Newly Invented
Pennsylvanian
Fireplace."*

Applications of Franklin's Invention

Although the stoves that use Franklin's name are not truly derived from his invention, many modern fireplace stoves and most inserts do owe their increased heat production to the basic principles he incorporated.

First of all, every one uses the principles of his heat shield to prevent warm room air from being lost during a low-burning or dying fire period. And due to the modern invention of heat-resistant glass—Franklin would have been delighted—it is no longer necessary to have an open fire to enjoy the sight of the flames.

Most important of all, however, the radiant heat of the fire—available through the glass in the form of infrared rays—is now vastly augmented by air heated by convection. In many units, furthermore, natural convection is given a helping hand with powerful fans and blowers.

The interesting thing about the various units is the ingenuity of the designers and engineers who have developed a number of different ways of applying this principle. You will see that some use outside ducting—some only for combustion; others only for convection—while many do not. Each is only too happy to explain and defend his design, and if you are interested, you can quickly learn enough from talking to them so that you may find yourself wanting to design your own unit. This is not as unlikely as it may sound; many good units on the market today were created by woodburners who were dissatisfied with what they were using and thought they could build something better.

TIP: IF YOU WANT TO INVENT IN A LESS CROWDED FIELD, CONSIDER CREATING A NEW WOOD-AND-COAL-BURNING UNIT. THERE ARE MANY GOOD ONES ALREADY ON THE MARKET, BUT THERE ALWAYS IS ROOM FOR ANOTHER ONE, AND TECHNOLOGY IN THIS AREA HAS BY NO MEANS REACHED THE PEAK OF ITS DEVELOPMENT.)

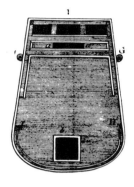

*Floor of firebox
of Franklin's Fireplace,
showing incoming
air passage openings
for combustion and
for convective air.*

*Franklin's Fireplace,
showing construction
of passages for
convective air;
shown flat and in
cut-away side view.*

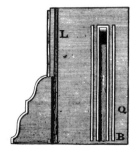

Stoves vs. Fireplaces

There are a few things you can do to make an open fire in a fireplace more efficient. You can add a fireback, you can add a specially designed grate, you can install a heat exchanger, and you can add glass doors. If you are planning to do all of those things, you might as well consider a fireplace insert, which puts them all together in a factory-built package. Manufacturers of most fireplace inserts claim the product will triple fireplace efficiency; that is, they say their unit is about 30–33 percent efficient. Some make much stronger claims, although, as I recall, the most anyone claims is about 50 percent efficiency.

In most instances, a freestanding wood- or coal-burning stove will outperform any fireplace unit; some have been rated 70–75 percent efficient in independent testing. There are many instances, however, when the homeowner does not want a wood stove. Most homes built within the last fifty years have small rooms; even living rooms are not as big as the old "parlors."

If you buy a wood stove that requires a 36-inch distance from combustibles, it may have to stand practically in the middle of the room to conform to safety standards. In the typical den or family room, even the middle of the room may not be far enough away from some of the walls, let alone the furniture.

On the other hand, one out of every three homes built today does have at least one fireplace. A fireplace stove or insert is a happy compromise between a freestanding stove and a fire in an open fireplace. It does not waste fuel. It cuts heating bills. You can still—with most units—enjoy a view of the fire. You have both radiant and convective heat and you can use the unit as much or as little as you want. A fireplace insert or built-in even looks like a fireplace, if that is important to you.

Part One

What Every Woodburner Needs to Know

2

Wood
The Best of All Fuels

Wood is the best of all fuels in many, many ways. In fact, as we will see, it has only one real disadvantage, labor; every other aspect of wood as an energy source is in its favor. Let's look at some facts.

Instant Availability

The consumer needs relief from high energy costs fast—not tomorrow, not ten years from now, not a hundred years from now, but today. Wood is here. Wood is above the ground. Wood is instantly available. If you buy a fireplace stove or insert today you'll have heat tonight. No negotiating with furnace or boiler men; no credit arrangements with (and subsequent dunning letters from) your local oil dealer; no indigestion every time you read the headlines in the morning paper.

Fast Pay-back Period

A fireplace stove or insert pays for itself the first couple of seasons—even sooner if you use it for the maximum amount of time and shop carefully when making your purchase. Using wood, instead of oil or electricity, is an obvious saving. Check how many gallons of oil you used last season, multiply it by this season's price per gallon (it's hard to keep up with increases; don't just take the price at the *beginning* of the season), and then compare it with the number of gallons you used once your stove or insert was installed. Add what you paid for wood. The difference between what the sole use of oil would have cost you and the actual expenditure for oil/wood use is what you saved. Compare this to the cost of your stove or unit and you will see how long it will take for your savings to pay for the stove.

Of course, you can slow up the pay-back process by running your unit inefficiently, by burning it as an open fireplace, by using it only as a decorative feature. I find, also, that many homeowners have used inserts to heat areas of the house—a family room or den, perhaps—that were never heated adequately. Or they are reveling in the luxury of a warm kitchen for the first time since they moved in, so they keep the fire going all the time, even though they had long since given up on heating that area with the oil furnace. In that case, it's not fair to compare, unless you are lowering the thermostat elsewhere and turning the fireplace area into a "keeping room"—the hub of activity for the household. On the other hand, wood heat is so delightful that people tend to gravitate to where it is; turning the heat down in other areas may be no hardship.

Low Maintenance

Fireplace stoves and inserts are uncomplicated. You don't need to call a serviceman; you don't need the overhead of an annual service contract (which gets more expensive every year). There are no moving parts (unless you have a blower, and you can usually replace that yourself) to get out of order. If you have installed your own insert—and most of them are homeowner-installed—you will find it easy to replace parts when necessary.

Dependability

Last winter, a homeowner I know had to have the oil company send a serviceman seven days in a row before the trouble with his burner was found and fixed. The oil company was very cooperative, but even so, a good part of each day was spent waiting for the man to come. The homeowner was tied to the freezing house—neglecting appointments, plans, and work—and was laid up with a cold for about ten days afterward. That simply would not happen with a wood stove.

Freedom from Power Outages

Unless you have a unit that cannot be operated without a blower, you will have heat even if a power breakdown has knocked out your central heating system. And if you do need electricity to operate your blower, a backup system—such as the Hydroguard—will provide the small amount of power you need to run the blower and a few electric lights until the power comes back on. If your auxiliary power unit has been hooked up to your central heating system, you are in even better shape.

Wood Is American

It's our wood grown right in our country. With wood there is no demeaning dependence on foreign sources and unreasonable governments. No one can hold a loaded wooden gun to our heads; we have all we need and to spare.

Wood Is a Cottage Industry

Many people are concerned about the size of some American companies and the control they are able to exert over the supply of their product: the American concepts of free enterprise and supply and demand no longer seem to operate with many of these products. But there's simply not enough profit in wood as a fuel to attract the major companies—at least, not yet. It's up to the consumer to be watchful and to make sure that wood fuel does not become big business, like oil, or even paper and pulp products. It's up to the consumer to demand that the government start now—at the beginning, when it is easier —to ensure that forest land, which is still largely in private hands, is not bought up by conglomerates and removed from the American citizens, to whom it properly belongs. We, the individual American taxpayers, have lost control of most of our natural resources; let's at least keep wood for all of us, rather than handing it on a golden platter to big industry.

Wood Means Jobs

The gathering and supplying of wood is presently in the hands of individuals and very small business enterprises run by two or three people. It is providing opportunities for jobs that are independent of big corporations. The individual who does not want to work for a big company now has the option of developing a wood-fuel supply business—or working for one. This is healthful for both the economy and the consumer—just as the small "truck" farmer is a better, cheaper, and more efficient producer of vegetables than the large, single-crop giant farm "industries." (If you question this statement about small vegetable farms, ask the Department of Agriculture; they did a study which—much to their surprise—showed this to be true.)

You Can Grow Your Own Wood

Not everyone can—it does take a bit of land—but many more people can have a woodlot than can have an oil well in their backyard (see Chapter 5: Managing Your Own Woodlot), and it's a natural for cooperative effort. Form a wood cooperative, combine small properties, and thumb your nose at the Persian Gulf.

Wood Is Nonpolluting

It never fails; whenever I give a lecture on wood heat, someone asks about wood pollution. And in the words of the old politician, I'm always glad to be asked that question.

Wood is the cleanest energy source we have. It's even cleaner than solar heat, because it doesn't use pollution-creating fossil fuels to produce the nonbiodegradable plastics that solar heat depends on.

It is true that carbon dioxide is released in the process of wood combustion, but it is no different—in quantity or content—from that released by wood that is left to decay and clutter the forest floor. Unlike the combustion product of fossil fuels, sulfur dioxide—a substance not normally found in nature—wood "pollution" is a natural product, and like so many of nature's carefully planned systems, it may be beneficial in some as yet undiscovered way.

Wood Ashes Are Useful

The "waste products" of wood combustion, ashes, are a valuable resource. They make an excellent fertilizer and soil conditioner. They are recommended by organic gardeners as a harmless pesticide dust, which discourages insects and garden pests without adding toxic substances to our vegetables. They can replace harmful salt as a winter help on icy driveways and walks. And if you want to try your hand at making your own soap, wood ashes are an essential ingredient.

Wood Is Renewable

We need never run out of wood. To quote the "New England Energy Congress Report": "Today we have the wood resources available to substitute for almost ½ of the 1975 oil consumption. By 1985 and later, given reasonable assumptions, we should be able to develop this resource to the point that 10–15% of our total energy requirements are met by wood. If an oil and gas shortage or significant price increases occur in the next decade, that contribution could be even greater. . . . Wood can be used to generate electricity, process steam, provide district heating, automobile fuel, and heat homes. . . . It can be used for two purposes currently consuming large quantities of oil—electricity generating and space heating."

At present, our forests are a mess. Cleaned up and properly managed, they can be a beautiful and productive source of firewood forever.

Wood Management Improves Our Forests

A recent letter in *The New York Times* stated: "The resulting ecological damage [of wood as fuel] is just too frightening to contemplate. . . . How . . . will humanity manage when we have chopped down all the trees in order to keep warm?" About a week later, a wood stove owner wrote in rebuttal, and shortly thereafter a professional forester set forth the facts for a concerned public.

Anyone who writes—or thinks—like the first letter writer simply does not know the facts. There is no ecological damage with proper forest management; on the contrary, there is only ecological benefit. Nor are we about to chop down all our trees; proper forest management increases the productivity of our forests; it does not deplete them.

To see the results of forest management, we have to look to Europe, since America has been wasteful and neglectful of its forests. Germany's Black Forest has been systematically harvested for over six hundred years. Today, just as beautiful as in the past, it is more productive and more welcoming to wildlife than ever before.

Finland—a model of sound forest management—has over 22 million hectares of productive forest land. It *has* to be productive, because wood and wood products are among Finland's leading exports, and have been for many hundreds of years. Finland was once in danger of depleting her forests, but wiser heads prevailed and forest management was taught to the individual landowners (most of Finland's forests are privately owned), so that today more wood is grown than ever before in the country's history. This is all the more impressive when you consider that Finland, part of which now belongs to Russia, has less land area than it used to.

If a tiny country like Finland, with its limited land area, can build a successful and thriving economy based on the continued cutting of its forests, certainly America can do as well or better. Even under the poor conditions that prevail today, one third of the United States—over 754 million acres—is forest land, and this is over 75 percent as much forest as greeted the first Pilgrim when he landed at Plymouth Rock.

Properly managed, that forest land will cool our country (forest land acts as an air conditioner and humidifer), encourage our wildlife (wildlife *increases* in managed forestland), restore our independence, and improve the quality of life.

The One Disadvantage

I have said that wood has only one real disadvantage. This is the labor of handling wood. Wood is heavy, bulky, and non-uniform. Stacking, lugging, and loading it into a fire requires that you be in better physical condition than many Americans. But wouldn't you like to be in better physical condition? A wood stove will help. Take it easy in the beginning and you may soon find that you enjoy working with wood. My personal pleasure is in stacking wood; once I start I find it hard to stop, and even with an aching back and tired arms, I still reach happily for "just one more log."

Summary

From every angle, wood is the best energy source we have. It is very versatile; it can be burned as logs, chips, sawdust, waste, etc. It is nonpolluting, renewable, and efficient. We have the technology for increasing production and can easily develop a distribution network because it is so widely available throughout the United States. The consumer will have to insist on the government's paying more attention to its wood resources and providing help such as it gives to fossil fuels; this will never happen unless taxpayers insist. There are no strong wood lobbies, because wood does not attract capital.

Wood doesn't mean biting the bullet, turning down thermostats, doing without; wood means cozy comfort and a better life, as well as a more beautiful America. If anyone asks you, "Why Wood?" ask them, "Why not?"

3

Types of Wood

There are basically just two types of wood, hard and soft. Usually, hardwood trees lose their leaves in the fall, and softwood trees have needles and don't lose them. As with all rules, there are exceptions, such as the tamarack, or larch, a softwood tree that in the winter is as bare as any locust. Hardwoods are much more desirable as fuel and you should burn mostly hardwood, unless you live in an area where it is not obtainable. In New Mexico, for example, piñon pine is most commonly burned because no other tree grows there in such quantity.

Hardwoods

Hardwoods are the better fuel for a number of reasons. They burn "cleaner" —that is, they will not cause as fast a creosote build-up and will generally smoke and spark less. High-rated hardwoods have excellent coaling qualities and will provide a longer burn. They are harder to ignite than softwoods, but once afire will burn steadily and at a more even temperature.

Hardwoods include many of our common trees—the hickories, the locusts, the oaks and beeches, ashes and maples. Even among the hardwoods, though, some are better than others.

The hardwoods with the highest BTU ratings are: butternut and shagbark hickory, black locust, ash, red and white oak, beech, yellow birch, hard and red maple, pecan, dogwood, ironwood, apple, walnut, and elm.

There are a few points to make about this list, however. Elm, in the words of an old poem, "Burns like the graveyard mold," and will smolder and smoke indefinitely no matter how dry it is. And while hard sugar maples make good firewood, weed maples are not in the same class.

The hardwoods that are next highest in BTU rating include: white birch, black cherry, green ash, red and silver maples.

Softwoods

Softwoods make excellent kindling because they ignite readily and burn hot; in small quantity, these are desirable characteristics. If, however, softwoods are your only source of firewood, you will have to manage your fire somewhat differently from a hardwood fire, and will have to add fuel much oftener. A softwood fire is much more difficult to hold overnight and the coals will die out much faster.

The most undesirable feature of softwood fuel is its high creosote build-up. If you burn much softwood, you should inspect your chimney several times a year for possible cleaning. Because softwoods spark, you are also much more liable to have a chimney fire.

Some softwoods are more desirable than others. High and medium rated in terms of BTU's are tamarack, or larch, Norway pine, southern yellow pine, Douglas fir, white cedar, red cedar, white pine, and ponderosa pine.

The Fragrant Woods

One way or another, there is always some smell from burning wood—even with an airtight freestanding stove. Perhaps it comes from the need to open the door occasionally for reloading. Perhaps an errant wind backpuffs through the draft control. You won't be able to enjoy fragrant woods in most fireplace stoves or inserts nearly so often, but you still may like to burn them once in a while. With an open fire, fragrant woods are a joy.

As a general rule, the fragrant woods are the ones that bear nuts and fruits. Apple and cherry are especially delightful and, because of their fragrance, are often used for smoking meats.

Occasionally, you will happen upon a wood that has an unpleasant odor. I have been told that black locust has such a smell when it is green, but since I don't burn green wood, I have never tried it out; it definitely does not have an odor when it is dry.

A bit of softwood kindling on top of your fire will also give off a pleasant piny scent. It makes a perky fire, too, with more sparks and crackling. Just don't get carried away; remember the disadvantages just discussed. If you are looking for sparks, cedar, Douglas fir, and hemlock will give you the most.

Driftwood

Driftwood snaps and crackles like softwood even if it's oak or locust. It is usually quite dry overall, but still contains pockets of moisture which cause the sound. It is a little awkward to manage sometimes, because of its irregularity of shape, but a chain saw can soon reduce it to manageable pieces and it can be a welcome addition to the woodpile. Some manufacturers, however, say not to use driftwood in their units; always read the owner's manual, especially with reference to fuel restrictions.

Field Guides

It's a good idea to acquire a working knowledge of what the various woods in your area look like. If you buy wood, you may come to depend on an honest dealer to give you a fair shake, but you may have a few unsuccessful encounters with ignorant or dishonest dealers before you get set; your best protection is a little knowledge.

If you plan to cut or collect your wood from the forest, it is essential that you know what you are choosing. Getting wood out of a forest is a lot of work and you would be foolish to put all that effort into a load of low-grade soft-wood.

There are several ways to learn to recognize wood. If the tree is standing, you have three clues; the silhouette, the leaves, and the bark. (There are others, but these three will probably be all you need to know for your purposes.) The silhouette is most useful in winter; the leaves and bark in summer. If the wood is cut, and in logs or split, you can look at the bark and the grain (easier to see in split wood). A field guide to trees is essential; base your selection on what you need to know for the way you are acquiring your wood. A bark and grain guide is very important for a novice buying wood from an unknown dealer.

4

The Consumer's Guide to Buying Firewood

Units of Measurement

It would be much better for the buyer if wood were sold by the pound; pound for pound, all types of wood deliver the same number of BTU's. Hardwood is heavier than softwood, and some hardwoods are heavier than others. Paying by the pound would be a much more scientific measurement, but most wood isn't sold that way, so we have to deal with the customs of the trade. Wood is usually sold by volume and the terms "cord," "face cord," "rick," and some others you may run into have fairly precise definitions.

Cord

A cord of wood measures 128 cubic feet; it is usually described as a stack of cut wood 4 feet wide by 4 feet deep by 8 feet long. That sounds clear enough, but actually, most people don't buy firewood in 4-foot lengths. They don't want the labor of cutting it to the 18-inch or 24-inch lengths needed for their stove or insert. If, however, you order a cord of wood, cut to any length you specify, you have a right to expect the stack to measure the full 128 cubic feet.

Face Cord

Technically, a face cord is wood cut to shorter than 4-foot lengths. If, for instance, you need 16-inch logs, you may be offered a face cord, which should stack to measure 4 feet by 8 feet by 16 inches. Unfortunately, that adds up to about one third of a standard cord, which means a lot less wood. Be sure you and the wood dealer are communicating. When you order a full cord, always add "128 cubic feet."

Run/Rick

These are other terms for face cord.

Truckload

Beware of dealers who sell wood by the truckload. Some trucks can't carry anything like a cord of wood; some can carry five or six cords; really large trucks hold up to ten cords. A cord of seasoned hardwood weighs roughly two tons; obviously, it can't come in a United Parcel Service panel truck, or even in the typical pickup truck.

Once you have determined visually that the truck is large enough to carry two tons, you still have no way of knowing whether the pile dumped onto your lawn is a full cord. We'll tell you how to deal with that below.

Unit

A unit is the amount of wood you can carry in the average large American station wagon without destroying the springs when you go over the first bump or into the first pothole; it doesn't mean loading the wagon up to the ceiling. What it usually adds up to is the equivalent of a stack of 16-inch wood 2 feet by 2 feet.

Don't buy wood this way; it makes you look like a novice and it won't last long enough to be worth the work of picking it up. You'll be buying about 1/24 of a cord and paying a premium price for it.

Cord

Always buy at least one cord of wood at a time. Your first problem is to determine whether the amount of wood delivered is a whole cord. To do this, you have to have it stacked, either by the person delivering wood (impractical —he's usually got better things to do with his time), by a high school student (also impractical—you never know exactly when the wood will be delivered and you have to pay the student by the hour), or by you and your family.

Stacking wood is fun, but don't put it off; stack it as soon as possible so you can get back to the dealer if it is short of a cord. If it is short, it doesn't mean the dealer is a crook; he has made an estimate of how much wood he is dumping and he may easily dump a little more or less than a full cord. A reliable dealer will make good on shortages if you call him promptly. Even wood-stove retailers and other "commercial" users of firewood often have to call about a shortage. Once you get to know and trust your wood dealer, it's usually enough to call and tell him how much he is short and ask to have it made up with the next delivery. It's a good idea, in that case, to remind him about the extra wood he owes you the next time you order.

Buying by the Log

If you don't mind the work of splitting the wood, buying by the log should get you a better price (you save the dealer labor), and it stacks more quickly. Some people seem to think they can stack split wood more *closely* and will therefore get more in a cord of split wood than in a cord of logs. I tried this out with two batches of wood and decided that the tightest way to stack the split wood was by putting the split edges together. When I was all finished, I took a look and realized that what I had done was make logs out of the split wood—only they tended to separate a little so they took up more room than the whole logs would have. If you think you can do better, try it out.

Most people I know would rather not have to split the wood they buy; they save that labor for wood they get free. It depends partly on the area in which you live. If dealers are used to delivering it split, they won't give you as much of a price break on logs as they should. In Maine or similar wood country, on the other hand, they'll charge a stiff premium to the sissy who won't split his own wood.

Buying by the Stack

If you visit the dealer to inspect the wood he has for sale, you may find it stacked one of two ways: with all the logs horizontal, or with every row at right angles to the row beneath. The only stack you should be interested in is the first. Stacking the second way is great for drying green wood—in fact, it's the only way green wood should be stacked—but it's not proper for measuring to determine a cord.

Even horizontally stacked wood can be stacked too loosely. The old New England rule for stacking wood goes something like this: "If you're selling, stack it so a cat can run through. If you're buying, stack it so it can't." Let the buyer beware.

Specifying Types of Wood

Ideally, you would like to buy a cord of oak, locust, or hickory and nothing else. Unfortunately, trees do not grow that way. Most dealers have access to a mixed bag of wood and the best you can usually do is specify mixed hardwoods, no elm. Elm is easily recognized and you should learn to spot this one wood, if no others. Since elms are frequently cut down because they are diseased, it is entirely possible for a small dealer to try to sell you a whole cord of elm. I had a dealer do this to me once and he had it dumped before I came out and saw what he had done. He took it all back, of course, but I think he honestly didn't know why I didn't want it.

If you specify mixed hardwoods, don't accept any pine or cedar or other softwood. If you do, you're paying filet mignon prices for hamburger.

Payment

Wood is sold on a cash basis; payment on delivery. I always pay by check, however, which gives me a certain amount of leeway in case I discover something wrong when I am stacking the load. Stopping payment on a check will usually mean you've done your last business transaction with that wood dealer, so don't do it unless you think you have really been cheated. There are many honest mistakes made in the fuelwood business and you should assume ignorance, not greed, is the dealer's problem. A phone call to him will soon tell you whether he is willing to make good or not.

Green Wood

When ordering, specify seasoned hardwood, rather than just hardwood. Green hardwood won't be suitable for burning for six months to a year. If you're desperate you can burn it after three months, but you won't get your money's worth.

If you are buying your wood six months before you will need it, you may be willing to buy it green and season it yourself. In that case, it should cost you less than seasoned wood.

If you buy green wood as whole logs, split it yourself as soon as you can. I don't mean make a marathon chore out of it, but split wood will dry out faster and that might be important.

If you buy the logs larger than the size you need—4-foot logs for a 24-inch firebox, for example—you might want to cut them up while they are green. This is important with wood like black locust, which becomes very difficult to saw when dry.

Storing Firewood

Once you have bought your wood, the way you store it can make a difference in the burning.

Green wood, as we have seen, should be stacked differently from dry wood.

The woodpile should always be off the ground; a rough way to achieve this is to use some of the logs as a kind of platform—run them the opposite way to the way the pile is stacked.

If you have a choice, store your wood in the sun or under shelter. Many people tend to stack their wood against or between trees, where they are in shade most of the day. Wood constantly reabsorbs and gives off moisture, and a shady spot will encourage the growth of mold, fungus, and insects.

If you keep it outdoors, cover it with plastic on rainy days. Thoroughly dry wood (which still retains about 20 percent moisture) will never be as difficult to burn as green wood unless it becomes thoroughly waterlogged, but rain doesn't do it any good and it takes only a minute to throw a piece of plastic over it. Take the plastic off when the sun comes out or the moisture will condense on the underside of the plastic and drip back onto the woodpile.

Don't store wood in the house or stacked against the house or garage. Cut wood attracts all sorts of undesirable insects; I have creosoted railroad ties outlining my driveway, and one fine sunny day, I discovered carpenter ants swarming all over one of them. Creosote is supposed to keep insects away, but apparently this particular batch of ants had developed a taste for it and had built an enormous nest in the ties.

Store rotted wood and sound wood separately. Rotted wood is not anything you would pay money for, but you may be able to collect quite a pile of it over the spring and summer. It won't give you the same heat as sound wood, but it's free and good for something. You ought to use it up as soon as possible, however, so keep a separate stack and combine with some sound wood when building your fire. If rotted wood has decomposed to the point where it is all crumbly, don't burn it. It is too valuable in the garden to use as firewood. Put it near your compost heap or just in an out-of-the-way corner until it decomposes enough to pick up with a shovel and spread as topsoil.

You ought to have an idea of how much wood you have in a pile; for instance, you might need to be able to tell whether you will need to order more before the end of the season. Some people like to build wood bins that hold a specific amount of stacked wood; then they can tell at a glance how much is left. If the bin holds four cords and it's half full, obviously two cords are left. You may not have the room for four cords in any one spot, so instead make standard—such as one cord—stacks wherever it's convenient. You can contain the wood with four pipes, two on either end of the stack, and make them just the right height to hold your cord (which will vary in size depending on the length of your logs).

How to Get Wood Free

Your own woodlot is the best source of free wood, but even a small piece of property will have occasional windfalls. After a storm, you can pick up kindling, if nothing else.

If you live near the beach, collect driftwood. You will get excellent exercise and it can easily turn into a favorite family outing. Don't be surprised if an occasional piece turns out to be a sculpture you don't want to part with.

The banks of rivers, ponds, lakes, and swampland are all good sources of fallen wood. You will find especially good hunting in the spring, when the frost-heaved roots give way as the ground turns to mud. Be sure to get permission to cut wood on public or private property; it's not usually difficult and you are performing a service.

In some areas, such as Connecticut, there is comparatively little state forest and usually a long waiting list for permits. Don't let that stop you from putting your name on the list; your turn will come sooner or later.

Call the telephone company and ask their schedule for pruning. They must do this periodically in order to keep the wires clear. Usually the work is contracted out and you may be referred to the tree company that does the actual cutting. They may give you schedules for surrounding towns as well as your own.

If you don't use your town dump, now is the time to get acquainted with it. The town hauls a lot of good firewood to the dump in the form of fallen or cut trees and you will be saving taxpayers money by retrieving it. Here again, make sure it is cleared with the proper authorities; the man supervising the dump is used to people scavaging for antiques, but he may be a little put out when you turn up with a chain saw.

Speaking of antiques, town dumps also contain usable wood in the form of old chairs, kitchen tables, and bookcases. Most of it is probably pine and should be used sparingly, but sometimes it's oak or walnut or something else beyond repair but not beyond burning. Old wooden bed frames are especially easy to cut up.

Ask your local lumberyard where they keep their scrap barrel. Avoid laminated pieces (plywood and the like) unless you have a unit that brags it will burn anything; you don't want an explosion in the firebox. Here, also, most of the scraps will be pine but great for kindling.

If you live near a town, look in the phone book for scrap metal dealers. If they buy engravings, they often have to take them off wooden blocks. These blocks are top-grade hardwood and no use at all to the scrap dealers; they remove the blocks from the engravings and toss them in a heap to be carted away. No reason you can't do the carting. Since most media have been gradually switching to printing processes that no longer use engravings, they are rapidly being disposed of. This is a source that won't exist in a few years.

TIP: EVEN IF YOU CAN GET WOODEN ORANGE CRATES, DON'T BURN THEM. FOR ONE THING, THEY MAKE TOO HOT A FIRE. FOR ANOTHER, THEY ARE COLLECTIBLES, ESPECIALLY IF THEY HAVE LABELS ON THEM, AND ARE WORTH MORE THAT WAY THAN AS FIREWOOD.

If you live near a furniture factory, check it out for scrap.

If you live in a logging area, talk to the foreman or owner or anyone who can give you permission to go in after the culls and branches and tops that aren't good for board lumber.

Wherever a new house is being built or there is remodeling, there is scrap lumber left lying all over the place. Speak to the foreman and ask him where his men leave the scrap (you don't want to get hauled in for removing materials from a construction site without permission). Explain what you want it for. Construction men hate to clean up; it's time-consuming. They will be delighted to have you do it for them if you do it after hours and don't get in their way.

Take a ride in the country after a storm. If you already live in the country, ride around your local roads. All the wood lying on the roadside in the form of fallen trees and branches is public property if it is within the roadside limits.

If you see wood fallen on private property (a big tree down, for example), ring the doorbell of the nearest house and ask if they would like you to remove it. As more and more people buy wood stoves, you'll get fewer and fewer takers. On the other hand, the owner may not want the work of cutting it up himself and may make a deal with you; your labor in exchange for a certain amount of the wood you cut.

5

Managing Your Own Woodlot

The reason wood is described as a renewable resource is that we can make more of it whenever we want. Unlike the fossil fuels, which take millions of years to form, a well-managed woodlot can produce a wood crop each and every year forever. If this idea seems strange to you, think of raising food crops; it seems perfectly ordinary that we raise wheat, corn, tomatoes, and other foods every year. As we learn better crop management and develop more prolific strains, we have even been able to increase our production of almost all these crops. Wood is no different.

How Much Land Do You Need?

If you wanted to use wood as your only source of heat, you would need about six to ten cords of hardwood a year. On the average, one acre of land will produce one cord of hardwood a year. This doesn't mean, of course, that each year you cut down all your trees and start over; obviously, it takes more than a year to grow a tree to harvestable size. What you do with that acre—as with any size woodlot—is cull each year the trees that have reached suitable size, leaving the others to continue growing. The effect would always be to leave woodland, and only you would know what had been culled out. If you are using wood for supplemental heating only—as a backup for solar heat or to cut down on the use of your central heating system—a cord of wood might be enough. With occasional fireplace use (using the efficient fireplace stoves, inserts, or built-ins), even a few trees harvested yearly could appreciably reduce the amount of wood you needed to buy or gather elsewhere.

Privately owned forest land is an important part of the whole wood supply picture. In Connecticut and New York, for example, approximately 85 percent of the forested areas (about 40 percent of the land in the two states) is privately owned by over 500,000 landowners. Most of these holdings are in parcels of under ten acres. If each one of these landowners were to take the wood crop seriously, we could greatly expand the production of wood. At present, much of that forest land is deteriorating because it is not cared for; managing it as woodlots would improve it aesthetically and environmentally, as well as productively.

If you own even a small parcel of land, you might want to use it to grow some wood—either to use or to sell. If your land borders other small parcels, it might be practical to get together with your neighbors and pool resources by going into a small woodlot "business." The amount of work involved is comparatively little and the profit margin is high.

How Would You Start?

Assuming you know nothing about woodlot management, where could you get advice and how would you start out?

First of all, it depends on whether your land is already wooded or is still pasture or given over to crops. Pasture, left to its own resources, will eventually become forest. By 1850, 80 percent of New England forest land had been cleared by the colonists and their descendents to create farmland. Today most of that land has been allowed to revert to its original form and the amount of farmland is dwindling every year. Chances are your land is forest land unless you have been maintaining it by clearing it regularly.

If Your Land Is Open Land

If all the trees have already been removed from your land, you will want to speed up the process of its reverting to forest by planting trees. This is not the arduous task it may appear to be. A local farmer can probably be found who will come in with a machine that digs the right kind of holes at appropriate distances. Seedlings can then be dropped in, either by machine or by hand, surrounded by earth and tamped down, watered, and left much to their own devices. You may have to protect them from deer and rabbits the first couple of winters and you may have to water occasionally in a drought, but most woodlot farmers settle for a certain percentage of loss—just as vegetable gardeners and orchard owners must—rather than put in the extra work to save each and every seedling.

TIP: IF YOU HAVE A FARMER HELP YOU, WATCH THAT HE DOESN'T PUT THE HOLES TOO CLOSE TOGETHER. THE TREES SHOULD BE PLANTED FAR ENOUGH APART SO THAT A HAYING MACHINE, OR AT LEAST A SIT-DOWN MOWER, CAN GET BETWEEN THE ROWS. REMEMBER THAT THEY WILL GROW AND THE BRANCHES WILL HAVE A CONSIDERABLE SPREAD. IF YOU DO NOT TAKE THIS PRECAUTION, BRAMBLES, HONEYSUCKLE AND OTHER VINES, AND TALL WEEDS CAN DESTROY YOUR ENTIRE PLANTING IN A FEW SEASONS. EVEN REASONABLY MATURE TREES CAN BE STRANGLED BY VINES, AND HANDCLEARING IS IMPRACTICAL. DON'T LEAVE IT TO THE FARMER'S JUDGMENT: FIND OUT THE CORRECT PLANTING DISTANCE AND MAKE SURE HE ADHERES TO IT.

If You Need Advice

Since it is unlikely that you are a trained forester, you should consult one about how to grow and manage your woodlot. To get the name of the forest ranger nearest you, call your local U.S. Department of Agriculture extension office. He will walk your property with you, advise what trees to plant (if any), what to cut, and how to manage your land so that you improve it at the same time that you crop it. If you have any doubts that planned cutting improves forest land, they will soon be dispelled. Forest rangers are delighted that forests are now being managed instead of being allowed to deteriorate through neglect.

Getting Seedlings at Bargain Prices

The United States Government is happy to help landowners plant trees and shrubs, and a special program makes this possible at a nominal cost. Ask your local U.S.D.A. extension service to send you information on the next sale. You can buy many different kinds of seedlings and you can be sure they will be of good quality and exactly what you have ordered. The cost is so little that it will amaze you.

Getting Seedlings Free

Some of the trees that are most desirable for firewood are also self-perpetuating. A particularly good example of this is the black locust. This tree has a number of shallow roots that radiate just below the surface of the ground in a horizontal direction. When you cut down a black locust, seedlings spring up all along these roots, and cutting down one tree can create a tiny forest the very first season. You will also find that a few black locust trees in the vicinity will result in seedlings cropping up every year in all open ground. I have to keep rooting them out of my vegetable garden, my lawn, and my bit of open meadow; I even have one growing just above the septic tank. Up until a few years ago, I used to mow them down as nuisance trees (I already have a grove and that was enough), but now that I appreciate their wood production, I transplant the seedlings to an out-of-the-way spot and share them with towns-people who are not lucky enough to have any on their property.

There are many other trees that propagate themselves in this fashion; your forest ranger can tell you which ones are available in your part of the country.

What Kind of Trees Should You Encourage?

Here again, your forest ranger knows local conditions and can best advise you. He will also tailor his advice to the sort of forest you already have (assuming you have one).

In the beginning, if your woodland is typical of most woodland in New England, you will mostly be culling out undesirable trees—undesirable in terms of an ideal forest but excellent for burning.

Your first cuttings will be dead wood, either still standing or fallen. Partially rotted wood can be used as well as sound dead wood. Once you have used up all dead wood, start culling weed trees. Weed trees will outgrow more desirable types of trees and will soon smother them so that they disappear.

After weed trees, the forest ranger will show you how to thin out the woods to allow faster, healthier growth of remaining trees. At some point, he will recommend planting seedlings to replace trees you will be cutting in years to come.

Until recent times, you might have wanted to reserve some of the straighter, taller, larger hardwood trees for board lumber (which would still have given you a valuable firewood harvest of tops, cull logs, and branches), but today compare the value of a tree as board lumber to what you could get selling it as firewood. In some areas, you can get a higher price for the firewood.

Getting down to specific types of trees, I'm a big booster of black locust. It is a beautiful tree, loaded in its season with lovely white flowers, so richly perfumed that stepping into the late-spring night is like walking into a deliciously perfumed room. It is tall and slender in growth, reaching over 75 feet in height at maturity. Black locust is not only a hardwood, it is one of the best, providing 24,100,000 BTU's per cord of wood—more than any other wood, except shagbark hickory (which equals but does not surpass it). Unlike hickory, which—like most hardwoods—grows comparatively slowly, black locust grows over four feet a year. Although it grows tall, it stays slender until a considerable age, so it is easy to cut down.

TIP: IF YOU GROW BLACK LOCUST FOR FIREWOOD, BUCK IT TO SIZE SOON AFTER CUTTING. IT IS A VERY DURABLE WOOD, IDEAL FOR FENCE POSTS AND SIMILAR USES BECAUSE IT DOESN'T ROT EASILY, AND THIS QUALITY MAKES IT HARD TO CUT ONCE IT DRIES OUT AFTER CUTTING. SAWING A BLACK LOCUST THAT HAS BEEN WAITING AROUND FOR SIX MONTHS OR SO IS LIKE TRYING TO SAW AN IRON BAR.

Eucalyptus trees are being farmed by the Department of Energy, which has a plantation in Hawaii of 850 acres, with the trees planted at the rate of 2,000 per acre. They plan to add about 400,000 seedlings a year for the next seven years and will then harvest some of the trees to see how they work out as fuel. The idea is to chip the wood and use it as a substitute for fuel oil in power plants. If this works, it would free much local wood, currently being used by power plants, for domestic use. It might be that eucalyptus seedlings will be available for local woodlots. Try to keep up with developments of this sort; there are bound to be many changes in the next few years and the alert consumer will be the first to benefit from them. At present, most of the eucalyptus trees grown in this country are in California.

You may have heard of the "supertrees" that are being developed by some of the paper companies and other industrial users of wood. These are, unfortunately, pine trees. If, however, you live in the South—particularly the Southwest, as New Mexico—you are probably burning mostly pine anyhow, so these trees may be of interest to you. Watch for news items about them and write the companies that are carrying on the research. You could ask if it would be possible for you to purchase some seedlings of this new type for your woodlot. Most of these companies are sensitive about their forest management techniques and might be very amenable to selling—or even giving—you some seedlings, welcoming this addition to their public relations program.

Summary

In this chapter, I have only brushed the surface of the subject of woodlot management; it would require a book of its own to cover it fully. If you are interested in looking into the possibility of growing at least some of your own firewood, I strongly urge you to at least chat with your local forest ranger. He might even be able to steer you to a government program that would help pay for some of the expenses incurred in converting a portion of your land to an efficient woodlot.

In addition, you might write:

The American Tree Farm System
American Forest Institute
1619 Massachusetts Avenue, N.W.
Washington, D.C. 20036

They will provide you with a wealth of information and technical advice. Just remember they are industry oriented, rather than consumer oriented, and you will have to wade through a certain amount of self-serving chitchat.

6

Tips on Building and Maintaining a Wood Fire

A wood fire is part science and part art. There are certain rules to follow that will minimize problems, but wood does not come in uniform shapes, density, or degree of moisture content. There are many variables and each log of wood must, to some extent, be treated as an individual with its own peculiarities. The art is in recognizing how your fire is acting, and in being able to make a reasonably accurate guess as to what—if anything—to do about it. We all know some people can correct a smoking wood fire with one touch of the poker, while others will spend ten minutes readjusting the position of the logs and end up making matters worse.

Be Sure the Damper Is Open

This may sound like the repairman who tells the housewife to check and make sure her appliance is plugged in, an unlikely situation but one that happens all the time; people forget to open the damper. With most inserts and units the damper is never closed, so this is not a problem, but if you are using stoves or grates, firebacks, etc., keep the damper in mind.

Follow the ABC's in Building the Fire

A. Put down crumpled paper, not too much but *tightly* crumpled. Newspaper works fine.
B. Top the paper with kindling. Don't be stingy with kindling; it has to burn long enough to ignite your logs.
C. Place three logs on top of the kindling. These can be placed horizontally, with just enough space between the logs to allow a draft to come through. If placed vertically, tepee fashion, logs should touch at the top; the draft will take care of itself.

Use Only Dry Materials

Everything—paper, kindling, and logs—should be as dry as possible. Wet materials are not only harder to ignite; they will also take longer to produce heat because the fire will have to use the heat to drive off the moisture before it can make the fire hot enough to be heat-productive. If you have some seasoned wood and some green wood, do not use any green wood when starting the fire. Use it for when the fire is burning steadily and just needs an occasional log added.

How to Test Wood for Dryness

There are two easy ways for even a novice to spot dry wood. Dry wood tends to "check." Look at the log ends and you will see cracks radiating from the center of the log. If the logs have been split, the cracks will be harder to find because wood tends to split along the cracks.

Another test for dry wood is the sound it makes when two logs are banged against each other. Green wood will make sort of a dull thud; dry wood makes a nice crisp, sharp sound. Once you have heard the two, you will remember the difference.

Start the Draft Before You Start the Fire

A cold chimney will not draw, but it takes surprisingly little to heat it up.

Just take a tightly twisted spill of paper, hold it over your logs, directly in line with the flue opening. Light it and watch the flame and smoke. As soon as it begins to go up the chimney in a straight line, light the paper beneath the kindling. On a very cold day, or if the chimney is on an outside wall, you may have to lay two or three spills on top of the logs and light them at the same time as the one you are holding. It's very easy and you will soon gain confidence in this system; it makes lighting a fire a much easier job and keeps the room from filling with smoke.

Keep Some Ashes on the Firebox Floor

When removing wood ash, don't take all of it. An ashbed not only produces a better fire; it holds the coals that may fall from the andirons or grate and keeps them alive much longer. An ashbed also protects the floor of the firebox from excessive heat.

Don't ever let the ash bed get so deep that it touches the grate, thereby shortening its life.

Use Andirons or a Grate

It's possible to build a fire directly on the floor of the firebox—this is done routinely with most wood stoves—but most fireplace fires will do better with a grate or andirons. The function of these devices is to allow air to circulate freely through the fire. Fire requires oxygen in order to burn; the more efficiently oxygen is delivered to your fire, the better it will burn. Wood stoves usually have an elaborate system of air controls—on the door, as interior baffles, as secondary air intakes—but some units require the woodburner to compensate for all of these by how well he manages the fire; a grate makes it easier.

Some grates are designed to hold the logs at special angles or separated in certain ways; the inventor of each of these thought he had created *the* ideal

28

*Tips on
Building
and
Maintaining
a Wood
Fire*

way to place the wood for fastest igniting and most complete combustion. Since the skill of the woodburner always plays a part in achieving success, you should try these out and see which one suits you best. They are comparatively inexpensive.

Read the Manufacturer's Instructions

Some of the more complex units have special instructions for building the fire. Following these instructions is much easier than learning by trial and error.

For example, here are the instructions for starting and maintaining a fire as they appear in the owner's manual for the Elite Fireplace Insert.

Please follow these steps, in order, when starting your initial fire.
1. Open the damper and draft shutter on the stove all the way.
2. Slide baffle completely forward.
3. Crumple newspaper and place on top of the grate.
4. Stack small pieces of dry kindling on top of the paper.
5. Light paper and close door.
6. After the fire is blazing, open door and gradually add large pieces until the fire is going strong enough to accept logs.
   CAUTION: DO NOT USE FLAMMABLE LIQUIDS, UNDER ANY CIRCUMSTANCES, TO START FIRES.
7. After the fire is burning well, with logs having been added, you may move sliding baffle further toward the rear and adjust flue damper and draft shutter as desired.

Experimenting with these controls will dictate the best settings for your particular heating requirements.

As you can see from these instructions, the procedure is different from what even an experienced woodburner might expect. Even with these specific instructions, however, you will notice the woodburner's art is still an important factor, as the last note indicates.

Never Overload the Fire

Too much fuel means too high and too hot a fire. The object is not a roaring blaze but a happy combination of flames and coals (wood). If you make too hot a fire, you will increase the draft and send more of the heat up the chimney. A properly managed fire will create more heat for the inside of the home and get the most out of your fuel. Always keep in mind the principles of combustion and go with them, not against them.

Principles of Combustion: How Wood Burns

Technically, wood does not burn. What burns is the volatiles and charcoal that are created. That is why wood will not catch on fire immediately when you put a match to it; it has to first undergo the chemical changes that create the volatiles, and a match does not create enough heat to activate the process. As kindling and paper evaporate the moisture in the wood, the wood absorbs heat. At a certain point, gases are given off and when these volatiles reach 480 degrees F., or the "flash point," as it is called, they will burst into flame if sufficient oxygen is present. The volatiles give off more heat than does charcoal, which is why a fire with flames (which burn the volatiles) produces more heat than one that is all charcoal.

Since the volatiles are gases and since heat rises, taking the gases with it, it is very easy to create a situation in which most of the volatiles go up the chimney almost as soon as they are produced. This is what happens with a roaring fire and, to a lesser extent, with an open fire. One of the reasons (but only one) that a freestanding wood stove produces more heat than an open fire is that the volatiles are contained within the firebox and are not so quickly dissipated up the chimney. A stove that is baffled is merely one that has interior construction designed to keep the volatiles in the firebox longer; the longer they are in the firebox, the more completely they burn. The more completely they burn, the more heat is produced. It's that simple.

Since the flames burn the volatiles and produce heat, the ideal situation is the longest possible flame path. As soon as woodburners understood this, they tried to devise ways of making the flame path longer than in an ordinary open fire. Even though the role of oxygen in combustion was not understood in Ben Franklin's time, Franklin did realize the importance of more completely burned volatiles. His solution was to try to invent a downdraft stove—one that sent the volatiles back down through the fire—but he never succeeded in getting one to work. A downdraft goes against the nature of volatiles, which is to rise. In more recent times, there have been some successful downdraft —or partial downdraft—stoves created, and some of the fireplace stoves and units utilize this principle. Ideally, it would be best if the volatiles could be redirected down through the fire several times, until they were almost totally consumed. This would not only make the maximum use of the heat potential of the wood; it would reduce creosote build-up to almost zero. Perhaps some-day an ingenious inventor will design a unit that does this; so far no one has been able to.

Moisture and Combustion

As we have seen, dry wood ignites faster and burns better—with higher heat production—than wet or green wood. The difference between the amount of heat produced by dry wood and green wood is so great that a dry softwood of good grade will produce more heat than green hardwood. Green white ash, for instance, is not as good a fuel as dry tamarack.

The reason for the superiority of dry wood is easy to understand. Heat cannot be produced until moisture has been driven off. Since even so-called seasoned dry wood contains approximately 20 percent moisture, it takes time for any fire to begin producing usuable heat. Wet wood, which can have a moisture content of over 100 percent (due to the way moisture is measured), will take that much longer to produce heat. Meanwhile, the fire will produce smoke and creosote and very little heat. This was brought sharply to my attention when I installed my first wood stove. To my surprise and delight, I found it comfortably heated eight rooms, where I had expected to heat only two or three. After some time, when I had someone helping me run the fire, I suddenly noticed that the house was chilly. We added more wood and ad-justed the draft controls, but nothing we did seemed to help. It finally occurred to me to check the woodpile. My friend had been getting green wood from a stack that was drying, instead of from the dry-wood stack. The difference the green wood made was so dramatic I will never forget it.

Part Two

What Every Coalburner Needs to Know

7

Heating with Coal

From the nineteenth century until well into the twentieth, coal was the most widely used fuel—for boats and trains, for steel mills, for public utilities, for domestic heat. It had replaced wood because it was more compact, easier to transport, required less storage space, was longer burning, and was generally handier and more desirable in every way except one; it was more polluting.

Even in Great Britain and Europe, where wood was generally too precious a commodity to be used for fuel, the pollution resulting from coal was a subject for concern. The famous London fogs were due in large part to coal burning, and writers in eighteenth- and nineteenth-century London complained bitterly of the effects of the acrid, coal-polluted air.

Ben Franklin, in his essay on smoky chimneys, mentions in passing:

> There is extant in the records of one of Queen Elizabeth's parliaments, a motion made by a member, reciting, "That many dyers, brewers, smiths and other artificers of London had of late taken to the use of pitcoal for their fires, instead of wood, which filled the air with noxious vapors and smoke, very prejudicial to the health, particularly of persons coming out of the country;" and therefore moving "that such a law might pass to prohibit the use of such fuel (at least during the session of Parliament) by those artificers." It seems it was not then commonly used in private houses. It's supposed unwholesomeness was an objection.

Coal is plentiful in many parts of the world, but it is especially so in the United States, where one third to one half (estimates differ) of the world's coal resources are located. Thirty-seven of our fifty states contain coal-burning strata, although the most desirable form, anthracite, is found mostly in a comparatively small section of Pennsylvania.

Coal was known to the American Indians, who spoke of it to the colonists, but wood remained the fuel of choice until the invention of the steam engine, which required the longer burn time and the more intense heat that coal provides. The coal industry, however, remained backward in technology, and as late as the 1940's, coal was still mined primarily by the arduous pick-and-shovel method.

Today, coal-mining techniques are much improved and the United States miner is able to produce more coal than can his counterpart in any other country. The Bethlehem Steel Company, one of the ten largest coal producers in the nation, estimates that the United States mines nearly 700 million tons a year—enough to fill a train that would reach three times around the earth at the equator. This is only a small part of the estimated three trillion tons of

33

coal that lie beneath American soil, a supply that could, at the present rate of use, make America fuel-independent for over 850 years.

Today, with the coal industry operating far below capacity, coal produces almost one half of our electricity and is used in the operation of some of our largest industries: pharmaceuticals, steel, concrete, paper, and food processing. Coal by-products, such as benzene, ammonia, light oil, and coal tar, provide the raw materials for synthetic fabrics, detergents, printing inks, fertilizers, dyes and varnishes, perfumes, food preservatives, plastics, weed killers, and many other products.

Increase in the use of coal would benefit our ailing railroad industry—since coal is usually most efficiently transported by rail—as well as provide employment for many skilled and unskilled workers in many fields and many parts of the country. In 1975, there were 170,000 men employed in the coal industry; even a modest increase in production would require an additional work force of 125,000 men by 1985. With coal mined and transported to capacity, employment would increase in much greater proportions. Coal can be transported by rail, barge, trucks, and pipeline; even with 75 percent delivered by rail, other forms of transportation would benefit from increased business.

In addition to a higher rate of employment, we would all benefit from a renewal of mass transportation, which should then become more widely available and cheaper (since the railroads and other carriers would receive large and steady revenues from their cargos of coal).

We would benefit most, of course, by the recovery of our independence; foreign oil-producing countries could no longer threaten to destroy our economy, and we would free our own extensive oil reserves for those areas where they are most useful. Careful management of our forests could extend their usefulness to infinity, stretching our coal and oil resources to well over a thousand years. With our record in science and technology, it is certain that long before we had exhausted our natural resources, we would have harnessed the sun and made solar energy an inexpensive and viable alternative for every home in the nation, and for office buildings, factories, and other industrial uses as well.

With these easy solutions to the energy crisis lying well within our present capabilities, it is baffling to watch the floundering of our federal energy effort and the failure of the government to take immediate action toward a sure and predictable independence from any foreign oil whatsoever. The coal-industry executives with whom I have spoken are cautious about how quickly they could increase production to its maximum, and dubious about how fast the transportation network could be revitalized, but they admit that the sooner they get the go-ahead from the government and from industry, the sooner they can get to work, and they feel strongly that the federal government must take a hand in helping the transportation networks to gear up for the coming influx of coal.

The "Plantress" stove, used by Florence Nightingale in her hospital at Balaklava, was manufactured by Smith and Wellstood, makers of the Esse Dragon.

8

What About Pollution?

Coal used as fuel and left to its own devices is incontestibly a serious pollutant. But all it would take to make coal acceptable in terms of pollution levels is money. Money doesn't seem to have prevented the nuclear industry from spawning plants all over the country; enormous outlays have been justified on the grounds of future benefits. Coal could do a lot better for a much smaller outlay.

The three major stack air pollutants in coal are nitrogen oxide, sulfur dioxide, and carbon dioxide. There are many studies currently under way to try to reduce or entirely eliminate these undesirable stack gases. In New England, major universities, such as MIT, are conducting extensive research on various ways of burning coal, as well as the development of solvents that would help neutralize the sulfur content in the softer coals. The University of Maine is studying exactly what effect these pollutants, and the resulting acid rain they cause, have on human beings, animals, and vegetation, and thirteen universities have joined together in the University Coal Research Consortium of the Northeast (UCERN) to exchange information and research results for more efficient and productive work in this field. In the Fall 1979 issue of *The Energy Forum,* Professor Jean Louis, a member of MIT's Energy Lab and director of UCERN, said: "We're very, very strong on clean utilization of coal. . . . We're a strong environmental group, a strong health-effects group, a strong combustion group, a strong conversion group . . . everything that is important for that theme." With that approach, clean coal cannot be in the too distant future.

The government, also, is not completely inactive in its consideration of coal pollution. Recently, Congress, through the House Committee on Science and Technology, issued a report prepared by the Congressional Office of Technology Assessment (OTA) that analyzed the risk/benefit ratio of increased use of coal.

According to the report, the OTA did not find that "any significant violations of existing environmental standards . . . would inevitably result from a substantial rise in coal use." They then appear to contradict themselves by stating that "some adverse environmental impacts are liable to occur with increased coal mining and combustion because of conscious economic trade-offs, lack of efficient control devices or insufficient enforcement of existing standards." The problems to which they addressed themselves included those in both the mining and the burning of coal. In other words, they looked into the impact on the environment of mining operations; the acid drainage that is part of the mining process; and the danger of ground-level subsidence (which has been a particularly serious problem in Great Britain), which takes place once a site has been abandoned. The burning of coal, with its "emissions of sulfur dioxide, nitrogen dioxide, carbon dioxide and fine particulates," adds noxious substances to an already overburdened atmosphere as well as a new danger to home heating. Since the health consequences from extensive use of coal range from undesirable climate changes (due to a build-up of carbon dioxide), to individual health problems arising from polluted air, to damage to wildlife, vegetation, and crops by acid rain, it is clear that the threat from coal is, so to speak, on the land and on the sea and in the air. The pollution could conceivably be so extensive as to be irreversible. In view of these findings, the statement with which this paragraph opens seems extraordinarily sanguine, but the optimistic OTA point of view lies apparently in the hope of further technological advances toward the production of clean coal, stricter government control, and higher standards of industrial coal use.

Technology already exists for clean coal burning by industry. Sulfur, for instance, can be largely eliminated by the installation of stack scrubbers. Unfortunately, this equipment is expensive to install, and many manufacturers and utilities are not sure they would reap sufficient financial benefits from converting to coal to make the investment in nonpollution equipment feasible. If utilities were not routinely allowed to pass on additional fuel costs, they might be less complacent about the constant increases in oil prices, and might be more willing to opt for a more economical fuel, like wood or coal, even if its use required a sizable initial outlay. Under the present system they have little incentive to operate efficiently; it is strangely un-American, in my opinion, to allow the utilities to pass on these costs in a manner which deters them from bestirring themselves to find a cheaper alternative. The fact that coal burning with scrubbers would benefit the consumer by resulting in cheaper prices (even if only eventually) doesn't mean much to a utility that can continue to make maximum profits in any case, and pass on any excessive costs (such as the price of oil) that may come its way. It would certainly be more patriotic to try to make do with America's rich natural resources, even if it were temporarily inconvenient financially—and probably the government would gladly lend a helping hand. After all, the government is—or should be —the American taxpayer, who is reeling under high oil prices and who would be better off helping to switch to wood and coal, even if it meant a small temporary rise in taxes instead of a steady 30 percent to 40 percent a year rise in running his automobile, heating his home, and turning on the television.

In addition to reducing coal pollution by elimination of noxious stack gases, there are methods of cleaning coal before it is burned. These processes are expensive at present, but research already in progress may one day make this a routine part of the mining operation.

Another area open to improvement is efficiency of combustion, which could reduce the quantity of oxides and particulates that are released.

The third and in some ways the most likely method of reducing pollution is to step up the study of transforming coal into gas or liquid fuel, removing the pollutants as part of the manufacturing process, so as to produce a clean end product.

There seems to be no way around the fact that coal is not as clean a fuel as wood—but in an age when we are rapidly lowering ecological standards nationwide, and when we are still debating whether or not to continue to develop nuclear plants (at the same time that we are forced to deliberately vent "small amounts" of radioactive krypton into the air because of dangerous conditions still obtaining at Three Mile Island), we have to weigh the use of coal against demeaning dependence on foreign oil and hazardous reliance on nuclear plants. From an ecological standpoint, it would be far better to rely on wood alone, until coal can be made to burn cleaner, but we might compromise by using wood where it is convenient and where distribution is not too difficult and costly, and confining the use of coal to domestic use and to those utilities and manufacturers that will install scrubbers and take other necessary antipollution steps as they are developed. If coal were to be returned to its former position of prominence as a national energy source, it would, perhaps, be easier to get funds for research to make it ecologically desirable, and America could once again regain its self-reliance on its own natural resources.

All the reasons why coal supplanted wood in the first place still exist today; one cannot blame the homeowner for wishing to ease the loss of almost effortless oil and electricity by turning to coal rather than to wood. I personally prefer wood in every way, but perhaps when I am older and enjoy physical work less, I, too, may be grateful for the greater ease of heating my home with coal; especially if by then I can do so without harming the environment.

Stockton and Darlington Railway, England 1825.

9

Types of Coal

Coal, like wood, is divided into two basic categories, hard and soft. Hard coal is called anthracite; soft coal includes semi-bituminous, bituminous, sub-bituminous, brown and lignite, and peat.

The harder the coal, the more carbon it contains and the greater its heating power. Carbon is found in many forms in nature besides coal; diamonds are the hardest form of carbon, graphite the softest.

Ash content, which displaces carbon, is undesirable because it does not add combustible material and, in addition, causes clinkering (see page 49). The higher the ash content, the greater the clinkering, especially if the ash has a high content of fusible impurities, such as lime.

Moisture in coal is just as undesirable as moisture in wood, and for the same reason; it retards heat production until it has been driven off. Some types of coal contain—and retain—more moisture than others.

Anthracite thus exhibits the most desirable characteristics of coal as fuel: it contains little ash, moisture, or sulfur; it burns with a smokeless flame; it contains over 80 percent fixed carbon, and it has a low ash content. It is most unfortunate, from an ecological standpoint especially, that it is also found in the least quantity of any type. This is understandable since it is at the end of the evolutionary process that creates coal; approximately ten inches of peat are needed to produce one inch of anthracite.

Here is how the various forms of coal compare in terms of fixed carbon:

anthracite	84+%
semi-bituminous	70–84%
bituminous	50–75%
lignite (Texas)	41+%
peat	13+%

Peat

Peat isn't technically coal, but it is in the process of becoming coal, and is usually included in any discussion of coal. I recently saw a newspaper advertisement, by a leading New York department store, offering to sell "Irish turf." The copy read: "It's the real McCoy. Burns in your fireplace with an aroma and flavor of the Old Sod. Close your eyes and you're in a cozy country cottage. 8 lbs. boxed as shown, $13.00." It was packaged in a replica of a little Irish cottage.

Peat burns very, very smoky and is the least desirable fuel. If, however, you have a nostalgic longing for it, ask your local nature center if it can be found in any of the swamps around your area; you can dig it and dry it for a lot less than thirteen dollars for eight pounds. It is called turf in Ireland, and is the common fuel for most of that country. Large areas of peat are found throughout the cold parts of the world, including South America; in warm climates, it does not form in such a way as to make satisfactory fuel.

Lignite

Lignite is peat that has had longer to develop. It is usually a brownish-black color and the vegetable matter, of which all coal is formed, has decomposed and compressed even more than in peat. It is the first stage in the formation of coal that is considered true coal.

Lignite provides comparatively little heat, although more than peat, and has a high moisture content (approximately 30 percent) and high volatiles content. It has a smoky burn. Do not attempt to store lignite out of doors; it tends to disintegrate when exposed to weathering.

Since lignite will crack and crumble as it dries out, it must be used very soon after it has been mined. As a result, it is usually available only in areas where lignite mines exist. An example of this in the United States is the extensive use of the rich lignite deposits of Texas, which, to quote *Forbes* magazine, "has precipitated a lignite scramble, with utilities and energy companies competing for lignite leases. For utilities and industrial consumers with lignite nearby, it can be the cheapest energy source." Since many companies mine their own from extensive lignite mine holdings, the consumer should benefit from power at a much lower price. It remains to be seen if the savings realized through the use of lignite are passed on to the consumer with the same speed with which the higher price of oil was reflected in consumer bills. It is estimated that the lignite deposits available in the United States could replace approximately 100 billion barrels of oil, which would give solar technology a breathing space and time to get its costs down to a viable level.

Brown Coal

Brown coal is sometimes considered the same as lignite, sometimes not; it is certainly very close. It, also, has a high moisture content, which causes it to check badly when dry so that it is liable to break up or crumble when handled. It is smoky and not long-burning.

Cannel Coal

Cannel coal is a low-rank coal that is very popular when used for an open fire; it produces the prettiest flames of any type of coal. The flames are long and their brightness gives this coal its name, which is derived from "candle." In Scotland it is called parrot coal, because it makes a companionable chattering noise while burning.

In certain forms, cannel coal has an attractive, shiny look, and this type is the form of coal that is polished and sold as jewelry under the name "jet." Jet was very popular among the Victorians and, with the renewed use of coal, may well have a revival as modern jewelry. Antique Victorian jet is not yet expensive and might be good to collect.

Cannel coal is not a high heat producer, but because it has always been popular as a fireplace fuel, you may find it easy to obtain where other coal is not. It can be dangerous, however, if used in an enclosed firebox, because it is high in volatiles and may explode as heat expands it. Under these circumstances, it will also create too large and too hot a fire, not easily controlled by the usual means.

Bituminous Coal

Bituminous is the most common of coals; there is much more of it than of anthracite. It is a better fuel than the coals previously mentioned—higher in heat value, lower in moisture content.

Geologists estimate that it took seven or more feet of compacted vegetable matter to form one foot of bituminous coal. It is widely distributed throughout most of the world. All of the coke that fuels our steel mills is made from bituminous coal; it is also used to generate electricity.

Bituminous is classed as a soft coal, and unless you live in a few very limited sections of the country, it is the best you can get from your coalyard at the present time. A form of bituminous known as block coal comes in large lumps or cubical blocks and is not suitable for the average coal-burning stove. If bituminous is all you can get from the coalyard, you might be better advised to buy anthracite from a stove dealer, even though he will probably charge a premium price for it. (Don't compare the price of a ton of anthracite with a ton of lignite.)

Anthracite Coal

Anthracite is the diamond of coals: the hardest, the oldest and most compressed, the highest heat producer, the cleanest, the longest-burning, the most lustrous. It has an estimated heating value of 12,000 to 15,000 BTU's per pound. Ecologists take note: it also has the lowest sulfur content. It doesn't disintegrate easily, stores well, is easy to handle, and is the most desirable coal to burn. There is also much less of it available. It is mined in only a few areas in Pennsylvania, and in a comparatively small deposit where Idaho, Nevada, and Utah meet. There is also some of it in Arkansas, at the edge of a large deposit of bituminous coal that extends beneath six states.

Since anthracite is in such comparatively short supply, be sure you will be able to obtain it before you purchase a coal-burning stove that requires it.

COAL TALK

When you go to purchase coal, you may run into terms different from any of the ones discussed in detail in this chapter. Here are some of the more common ones.

Banded coal. This is a descriptive term (you can actually see the banding) for certain kinds of bituminous coal. The bands are usually formed of bright coal, dull coal, and mother of coal, but for your purposes, all you really need to know is that it is bituminous and, therefore, soft coal.

Block coal. Bituminous coal that characteristically breaks into large lumps or blocks, or any coal of that size.

Bright coal. The name comes from its jet-black appearance, although it looks pitchy rather than lustrous. It is more compact than dull coal and breaks with a characteristic conchoidal fracture. It is bituminous or semi-bituminous.

Briquet coal. Not to be confused with the wood charcoal briquets you use for barbecues and cookouts. Charcoal briquets are made from hardwood, not from coal. Briquet coal is made from coal dust that has been compressed into briquets that may be burned like coal. They are uniform in shape, usually square or oval.

Char. A form of fuel created by incomplete combusion. Wood char is called charcoal; coal char is called coke.

Cherry coal. A type of bituminous coal, soft but noncaking, that burns steadily with a yellow flame.

Clean fuel. A term applied to coal with a low sulfur content, primarily anthracite. Actually, no coal is as clean a fuel as wood.

Coal apples. Anthracite is sometimes found in spheroidal pieces, from one quarter inch to ten inches in diameter; most coal apples are about the size of an egg. If you should find one of these curious objects among your coal, you might want to save it as a collector's item.

Coal ash. Coal ash is the noncombustible matter in coal; it is left over after the combustible matter has burned. As far as I know, it is a useless waste product; I do not think it is suitable as a fertilizer (as is wood ash), but perhaps a use will be found for it as coal comes into greater domestic consumption. Coal with a low ash content—that is, with the lowest percentage of noncombustible matter—is the most desirable. Studies are under way to reduce the ash content of high-ash coal.

Lean coal. A type of coal classed as semi-anthracite.

Earth coal. A term sometimes used interchangeably with "lignite." It is very similar in appearance and combustion characteristics.

Peat coal. Better than peat but not quite as high-ranked as lignite, peat coal is at an intermediate stage in its evolution to true coal. It is sometimes artificially manufactured by carbonizing peat.

Soft coal. Bituminous coal is the most common soft coal, but the term is applied to any of the lower-ranked coals. If possible, avoid soft coal in domestic use.

10

The Consumer's Guide to Buying Coal

Buying coal involves some of the same problems as buying wood; there are many different kinds and distribution is generally spotty, unless you live near a coal-mining section, such as Pennsylvania or Colorado. On the other hand, coal underlies the earth in thirty-seven states, so even if not all the mines are active at the moment, you may find that many of them will be sometime fairly soon. Also, distribution of coal will grow with increased demand; if you want coal, call around and ask for it so that the industry will begin to get feedback and know there are potential buyers for their product.

At present, there may be only one coalyard within a fifty-mile radius of where you live, so don't look just in your local phone directory. I found a yard in an adjoining town that not only sold coal by the ton but also was willing to deliver. If you are that lucky, you will need a coalbin handy to a cellar window equipped with a coal chute so that the truck can deliver the coal directly to your basement. If you don't want to store it in the basement, be sure you have some sort of covered bin put together before the coal arrives. Coal is dusty (even though it is washed by the mining company); don't plan to put it on the porch or too near a living area; a shed on the side of the garage might be a good solution if your fireplace is on that level. (See Storing Coal, below.)

Another source of coal is the dealer from whom you buy your fireplace stove or insert. (If you buy a unit direct from the factory, you can still buy your coal from a local dealer—he won't turn away the business.) The only catch is that the coal is often sold in 50-pound and 100-pound bags; you will pay a lot more for it than if you bought the same grade by the ton. Usually, however, the bagged coal is anthracite—a much better grade than the coal sold by the coalyard, so you may not mind overpaying somewhat for it. Also, bagged coal is easy to handle; you can buy a small amount at a time—only what you need rather than a whole ton; you don't have to store it and it tends to be cleaner. In the beginning, if you are unsure of yourself, it's also handy to have the dealer to talk to. He will give you advice and help solve any problems that may arise. If you are used to managing a wood fire, he will be able to tell you how a coal fire is different and how to manage it efficiently.

Carting coal at Newcastle, 1764. The cart was called a chaldron and came in various sizes; chaldrons held from 32 to 72 imperial bushels.

Comparing the Cost of Bagged and Loose Coal

Forty 50-pound bags of anthracite weigh 2,000 pounds and equal one ton of coal. To compare loose coal, sold by the ton, multiply the dealer's price for a 50-pound bag of coal by 40. Subtract the per ton price and the difference is the premium you are paying for buying it bagged. Strictly speaking, you ought to add the cost of picking it up yourself as against having it delivered; considering the price of gasoline, that might easily be several dollars more. Some stove dealers who carry bagged coal will deliver it, but there will be an additional charge.

Quality and Price

Just as with wood, hard coal costs more than soft coal; anthracite will be by far the most expensive. Lignite or brown coal, sub-bituminous and bituminous, cannel coal, will all be considerably cheaper. The cheaper coals are no bargain; they will not only burn dirtier, they will burn faster. Coal with 14,000 BTU's per pound is obviously worth more than coal with only 9,000 BTU's. Beware, however, of the dealer who sells soft coal at hard coal prices. He cannot plead ignorance, because he knows what he had to pay. It is only fair that you pay more, in terms of tons, for small quantities of coal neatly bagged, but you should not pay premium prices for poor-grade coal.

Shopping Around

You may think there are not enough sources for coal in your area to enable you to shop around, but it is very unlikely that such is the case. Even if there are only two coal stove dealers, selling bagged coal, some competition will exist between them and you should make the most of it.

Buying out of Season

If all the prices in your area are identical in season, check out-of-season prices. Turnover is important to a retailer, who always has money tied up in his stock and during the slow season would rather move the merchandise even if he has to take a smaller profit to do so.

Out of season may be different from when you might expect. In New York City, for example, the Board of Education, a heavy user of anthracite, buys at the end of the summer, because that's when prices are cheapest in that area. At this time, they buy their entire year's supply; otherwise, the out-of-season savings might be eroded by peak in-season prices or by price increases.

Buying Your Entire Requirement at One Time

If this is your first season, you will have to estimate your coal needs. After the first season, you will have a good idea of how much coal you use in an average season. Buy a little extra in case the winter is harder.

You will not only get a better price buying out of season, but you may also be able to do a bit of bargaining because you are buying a larger quantity. If you are having it delivered, you also ought to realize a quantity savings in the delivery charge, since it doesn't take appreciably longer to deliver a large load than a small one.

Sizes

Anthracite, the most desirable coal to buy, comes in a number of different sizes, ranging from approximately 2 $\frac{7}{16}$ inches in diameter to the size of a grain of rice. Size is designated by various names: stove coal, nut coal, pea coal, and so on, all the way down to rice coal. Incidentally, the nut used for sizing nut coal is the chestnut.

Stove coal, in spite of its name, is not usually recommended for domestic use; it ranges in size from 1 $\frac{5}{8}$ to 2 $\frac{7}{16}$ inches.

Nut coal is the most popular size for domestic use; it ranges in size from $\frac{13}{16}$ to 1 $\frac{5}{8}$ inches.

Pea coal is the next most popular size; it ranges from $\frac{9}{16}$ to $\frac{13}{16}$ inches.

Smaller sizes are not desirable because they will burn up too quickly. You will find that grates are usually spaced so as to accommodate either nut or pea sizes. Be sure, however, to read the manufacturer's literature carefully; some manufacturers specify the size their unit calls for. The USDA recommends nut coal if no other size is specified.

Storing Coal

Anthracite is the cleanest coal. Lower-rank coals create a lot of dust when moved or handled; this should be kept in mind when planning a storage area. Anthracite, too, will make a bit of a mess, though not nearly so much.

All soft coal should be stored under cover; if it gets wet, it will deteriorate rather quickly. Even anthracite does not benefit from alternate wetting and drying, as from rain or snow. If you store your coal outdoors, you need a completely enclosed area; a shed with one side open is not satisfactory.

Since it is not desirable to store wet coal on top of dry coal, you might want to have two storage bins. In this way, you will not risk a delivery of wet coal being dumped on top of your already dry storage.

If you have a choice, store your coal in the cellar or on the shady side of the house. It is best not to store it under conditions where the temperature rises to over 75 degrees F. If you store it in an enclosed outdoor shed, be sure you allow enough openings to let in fresh air on a hot summer's day.

In planning a storage area, the rule of thumb is that a 4-cubic-foot bin will hold about two tons of nut coal. How many bins you need will depend on how much you plan to use your coal-burning unit.

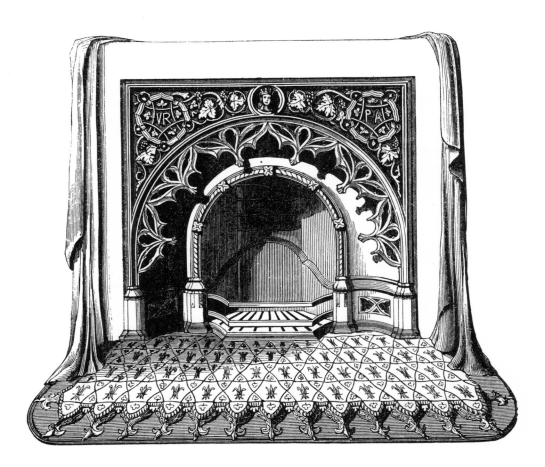

"From the manufactory of Messrs. Stuart and Smith, known as 'Roscoe Place,' Sheffield, an establishment which ranks high among those of that famous industrial town. [It is] made upon the principle known as 'Sylvester's,' whose invention formed an era in domestic economy and comfort. The superiority over old-fashioned grates has become widely tested by its very general use; these latter were so constructed that the larger portion of the heat passed up the chimney, from the fuel being placed so high, and, as a consequence, the cold, a condition directly opposed to health and comfort; it is obvious that the principle of construction must be best which throws the greatest heat where it is most required, and this is mainly effected by the invention of Mr. Sylvester. . . . The [one] in medieval style is designed by Mr. H. Duesbury, an architect of ability, who has shown much taste and ingenuity in adapting this style to its required purpose." FROM THE ART JOURNAL CATALOGUE AT THE CRYSTAL PALACE EXHIBITION, LONDON *1851*

11

How to Build and Manage a Coal Fire

An experienced woodburner is at more of a disadvantage in using coal than is a novice who has never used either solid fuel. Coal burns so differently from wood that a person who is used to wood not only has to learn about coal; he also has to unlearn many of the things he thinks he already knows.

The hardest thing to learn when switching from wood to coal is patience: coal simply does not respond as quickly as wood and you must allow for this factor in starting, tending, and banking a fire. As one coalburner put it: "The secret is *anticipation*. You must plan ahead how you want the fire to be at some future time."

The plus side of coal's slow response is that each stage is much longer lasting than a comparable stage with wood. If, for instance, you have been able to bank a wood fire for 8 to 10 hours, you will be delighted to find that a coal fire can be easily banked for 24 hours. This means that coal gives you greater freedom to be away from home, even with a comparatively small stove.

Coal also requires less physical labor. One to two buckets of coal a day are the most you ever will need. You may have a bit more ashes to dispose of, and you can't just spread them on the vegetable garden, but overall you will do much less lugging.

Starting the Fire

Coal is more difficult to ignite than wood and this must be taken into account when building the fire. Do not put any coal in the firebox at first.

Be sure the damper is fully open before you begin. Build a base with paper and kindling, just as if you were starting a wood fire, but with more kindling. Light a twist of paper and hold it over the kindling to heat the chimney and start the draft. As soon as the draft starts to draw the flame of the twist toward the chimney flue, light the paper under the kindling.

NEVER USE INFLAMMABLE MATERIALS SUCH AS GASOLINE, CHARCOAL LIGHTER, OR SIMILAR VOLATILE LIQUIDS TO START THE FIRE.

Once you have a good kindling fire, add a single layer of coal, enough to cover the grate. Remember, you should have the primary draft control fully open. When the coal ignites and is burning steadily with a blue flame (if anthracite) or a yellow flame (a soft coal), *gradually* add more coal. Be sure each new amount of coal has fully ignited before adding any additional; never completely cover the red coals.

If you add too much coal at a time, you may smother the fire, causing the formation of excess carbon dioxide, or you may cause back-puffing. Back-puffing may be caused, also, by windy conditions or a change in the nature of the draft in the stove (such as that caused by opening the loading door). This type of back-puffing is a nuisance but it is not serious. With coal, however, a more dangerous kind of back-puffing can be caused by adding fresh coals to the fire, even to an established fire. Since fresh coals give off larger quantities of volatiles, these may accumulate quickly over the fire and catch fire all at once. If this happens, too much pressure may be created and a back-puff, sometimes a small explosion, will occur within the firebox. Some coal-burning units, such as the Ashley Combination coal and wood heater, have a pressure relief outlet on the loading door to take care of this eventuality. Without such an outlet, the firebox can be damaged by this type of back-puffing. The Ashley manual suggests that you add no more than 10 pounds of coal at a time to their unit, to prevent the volatiles' building up in this fashion. If the unit you are using has a smaller firebox, 10 pounds might be too much to add.

Once the coals have caught, be sure to adjust the primary draft control and open the secondary draft control as much as is necessary. Many coal stove manufacturers do not completely trust the coalburner to exert proper care with secondary air and do not, therefore, make this adjustable; instead the secondary air inlet is fixed and delivers enough for safety at all times. The secondary draft control is essential to the safety of a coal fire since carbon monoxide will tend to form in the absence of secondary air. If you are burning primarily wood, you will want a secondary air intake that you can adjust; it will give you more control of the fire.

When burning coal, the object is to keep the basket grate filled (always providing, of course, that it is the proper size for the firebox). Take care that the fuel never comes above the top of the firebrick in a lined firebox. If the manufacturer has furnished the grate, it will probably be the right size, but if you have added a coal conversion kit, be sure that either it is designed to keep the coal below this level or you do so when adding coal. If the grate is one you have got from a source other than the manufacturer, as a coal conversion kit or basket grate, be especially careful in using it. *Do not use coal in any unit unless the manufacturer states specifically that his unit is designed to burn it.* As a rule, figure on a firebed about 8 inches deep.

Maintaining the Fire

Maintaining a coal fire is much easier than maintaining a wood fire because it requires refueling much less often. If you have switched from wood to coal, you will be amazed at how seldom you have to add fuel. One bucket of coal can conceivably last for twenty-four hours, depending on how the fire is run. At the very most, with a good fire maintained round the clock, you will never need more than two buckets in a twenty-four-hour period. If you are using excessive amounts of coal, either you are not managing your unit properly or you do not have a well-built unit or something is wrong with your fireplace/chimney construction.

One chore you have with coal that you do not have with wood is shaking the ashes and removing the clinkers that accumulate on the grate.

I have used the term "clinkers" and perhaps a word of explanation is due here. Clinkers never occur with a wood fire, only with coal. They are formed by ash material that is noncombustible. When impurities, such as lime, are present in the coal, the ash material joins with the impurities to form chunks that will not burn. The higher the grade or rank of coal, the fewer the impurities and the lower the ash content; a high grade such as anthracite will therefore form fewer clinkers.

If you have a good shaker grate, the kind that turns slightly and opens somewhat when shaken, most of the clinkers will fall into the ashpan. With a coal furnace, for instance, enough can be disposed of this way so that you do not have to concern yourself with those that remain above the grate until the end of the season, when you are cleaning out the furnace. In a small coal-burning unit, however, the clinkers may eventually become a problem. If you use a low-ranked coal, this problem will be compounded, and if in addition you do not have a shaker grate, you will eventually have to take steps to remove the clinkers manually.

I spoke to a number of people in the field about this and no one had a solution. Old-timers are used to an efficient shaker grate and have never had to deal with a fixed grate. Trial and error will show you the best way to deal with the particular setup you have. Since you will certainly not want to put the fire out in order to remove the clinkers, the first step is to learn to recognize that they have accumulated. They will never be *red* hot, like coal, and they will be very sharp to the touch. If you have a pair of fireplace tongs, from your open-fire days, you may use these to remove the clinkers one at a time. Add them to your covered ash bucket and handle it in the usual fashion.

One thing you can do to cut down on clinker formation is to avoid running too hot a fire. If a coal fire is burning too hot, it will almost liquefy the coal. As it cools off, these "coals" will look like cooling lava, because they have fused with impurities; these lava-like objects are the clinkers.

If you are familiar with cookouts—where the charcoal is ready for cooking over when all the coals have turned gray—you may tend to think a coal fire should be the same. It should not; occasionally, the ash must be shaken from the coals if you are to get maximum heat production. If you have a shaker grate, this is a very simple operation. If you do not, you will have to move the coals by poking them gently with a fireplace poker. You can get very proficient at this after a week or so of doing it.

Resist the temptation to shake the fire down too often; once or twice a day should be sufficient. Never shake down a large fire. Not only will you disturb the fire unnecessarily—and maybe put it out—but you are also liable to drop an excessive number of burning coals into the ashpan. The ashpan is not designed for this and you will shorten its life. In addition, you will waste good fuel, since the ashpan is not meant for heat production. Stop shaking as soon as red coals appear.

Empty the ashpan often enough to keep the air passage from the primary air intake in the clear; a coal fire needs a good draft of fresh air coming in under the grate. If you let the ashes build up too much, you may block part of this passage; you may also put stress on the grate.

When you are ready to add fresh coals, always open the damper fully before opening the loading door. Wait just a minute to let the draft get stronger and to avoid back-puffing.

The objective in running a coal fire is to keep it nice and steady. Fresh coal should always be added toward the back of the firebox. Pull some of the burning coals gently away from the back to create a depression; fill this depression with fresh coal. If you are not satisfied with the heat production from a good, steady fire, increase primary air intake gradually and also add a little more secondary air. Of course, your secondary air intake is already open—never run any sort of coal fire without it—but if it is adjustable, you can open it a little more at this time. With many units, such as the Petit Godin, the secondary air intake is not adjustable, but that needn't concern you, because the stove is designed for this mode of running the fire.

The importance of adding air when you add coal is due to the nature of coal combustion. As the coal burns, it forms carbon dioxide. Carbon dioxide is what you breathe out from your lungs and what trees and other vegetation give off at night. Carbon dioxide has a faint, slightly pungent smell and an acid taste. It does not support combustion, so your fire would go out if that were the only air present, especially since it is heavier than air and tends to settle toward the fire.

Unfortunately, as a coal fire that is producing carbon dioxide begins to run out of oxygen, the carbon dioxide turns to carbon monoxide. This is dangerous because carbon monoxide is extremely toxic and hard to detect. It is colorless, odorless, and tasteless. You are probably most familiar with carbon monoxide as automobile exhaust; it is also produced by gas ranges, mine explosions, burning electric installations, and iron or steel furnaces. Any carbon-containing fuel that is burned with insufficient oxygen can form carbon monoxide. It is very important to always make sure your coal fire is receiving sufficient oxygen to prevent carbon monoxide from being created; all coal-burning stoves should have secondary air intakes for this purpose. Carbon monoxide poisoning can be fatal.

Anthracite coal does not produce a long flame path; a steadily burning coal fire should burn with a short blue flame. Unlike a wood fire, most of the heat produced by a coal fire comes from the burning coals rather than from the burning volatiles. If you are used to a wood fire, and attempt to make your coal fire resemble it, you will waste fuel and lose heat. What you want to create is a fire with a deep fuel bed of red coals and blue flames licking just above the coals; that is the appearance of the most heat-productive coal fire.

Banking the Fire

If you want to slow down the fire—when you are going to bed at night or leaving for work in the morning—you will "bank" it. Experience will teach you whether enough coals remain to carry the fire over through the night or whether you need to add fresh coal. If you have been burning wood, you will soon learn that a coal fire has a much longer burn time.

In the event that you need to add fresh coal, add a little to the back, shaping the coal bed so that it slopes toward the loading door. The coals in the front of the bed, directly inside the loading door, should always be red and glowing; never cover these up. Some of the old-timers I have spoken with said that they "dampen" a going coal fire by sprinkling some ashes over part of it. It would be better if you had anticipated when you were going to bank the fire, and planned ahead of time to start letting it die down a little. When shaping the bed, disturb it as little as possible; if you bring ash to the top, you will create clinkers.

If you have added fresh coal, allow the fire to burn normally for at least fifteen minutes. You can then close the draft controls some, but *not as much as you would with a wood fire.* With a coal fire, the primary air control, the exhaust damper, and the secondary air intake must all be open *at least half-way* at all times. The object is to keep the draft in the firebox strong enough to prevent the fire from dying down so much that the carbon dioxide turns to carbon monoxide and seeps into the living areas. If the fire smolders, this is what will happen.

In the morning, you will be able to bring the fire up just by opening the drafts more. Once the fire is burning steadily, add a little fresh coal, as you would when maintaining the fire. Remember not to add too much and to adjust air intake as described in the foregoing section.

Ash Disposal

Coal ash should be treated like wood ash, with one difference. After it is placed in a metal container with as tight-fitting a lid as possible, so that any glowing coals will go out more quickly due to lack of oxygen, the bucket should be placed outdoors to minimize danger from carbon monoxide created by still glowing coals. You will find it a thrifty practice to sift ashes from a coal fire; sometimes the shaker grate will allow usable coal to fall into the ashpan and you can retrieve these by sifting. Watch your fingers; if the lumps are clinkers, rather than usuable coal, you may cut yourself. It's a good idea always to use heavy fireproof or fire-resistant gloves; coals stay hot much longer than you can imagine.

Do not scatter the ashes in flower or vegetable gardens. They may be used, however, on icy driveways. I would strongly suggest that you do not use them where people walk, because they cling to shoes and boots and will track up the house. If you plan to bury them, read the section on Ash Disposal in Chapter 15.

Exceptions

I have given you general rules for running a coal fire, but your unit may have certain special rules; read the manufacturer's manual to find out where you should vary from the standard procedure. For example, Proforma says to put the top air spin (secondary draft air intake) in a closed position and the flue damper in the fully opened position when loading on fresh coal. Proforma has a special downdraft system instead of the usual secondary air intake, and attempting to follow the standard procedure with their unit might create back-puffing, instead of preventing it. You might find it a good idea to underscore or check the sections in the owner's manual that contain specific instructions of this sort, and make it a practice to refer to them each time you manage the unit until you are doing them automatically. Always remember that a coal fire, if improperly managed, can be lethal.

Part Three

All About Solid-fuel Fireplace Stoves, Inserts, and Built-ins

12

Buying a Wood- or Coal-Burning Unit

There are three efficient ways to increase the heat production of a fireplace: with fireplace stoves, with inserts, and with built-ins. Accessories such as glass doors, firebacks, heat exchangers, and specially designed grates can be added to any fireplace, but they represent a fragmentary approach to the problem, although there is something to be said for the more sophisticated C-grates or hydronic grates, which often form the heart of more elaborately designed inserts and built-ins.

Each type of device has advantages, and there are many subgroups within the basic types. I cannot possibly cover all the variations, but here is a rundown of what you will usually encounter.

Fireplace Stoves

"Fireplace stoves" is not a clearly defined term, even within the industry itself. The consumer will meet with a certain amount of confusion on the part of the dealer. If, for instance, you ask to see a fireplace stove, you may be shown a Franklin type—a freestanding stove with doors that can be left open for viewing the open flames, or one with glass windows through which you can watch the fire.

For the purposes of this book, I have defined fireplace stoves as those designed to be set against the fireplace opening (with perhaps a panel sealing off the rest of the opening), or to be placed on the hearth and set slightly within the fireplace proper. Some of these are freestanding stoves that happen to sit low enough to fit into the fireplace; others are especially designed for this purpose.

The advantage of a fireplace stove over ordinary freestanding stoves is that it does not have to be set so far out into the room. At the same time, because it is virtually a true stove, it can provide almost as much heat—*almost* for two reasons:

First of all, installed against the opening, the back of the stove is not very heat productive because it heats only the closure panel behind it; whereas a completely freestanding stove—by virtue of being situated farther into the room—automatically heats a larger volume of air and objects.

Second, fireplace stoves that sit within the hearth give less heat because more of their surface is contained within the fireplace, rather than within the room as a whole. There is, however, some benefit obtained from their heating the masonry firebrick inside the fireplace. The firebrick absorbs heat from the stove and—unless the fireplace has a closure panel—sends it back into the room. The fireplace thus acts as a heat sink and radiates heat for a time even after the fire in the stove has died down. On the other hand, many of these stoves fit almost entirely within the fireplace, with most of the stove *behind the closure panel.* Most of these stoves—an example is the Moravian Fireplace Stove—incorporate a double-walled construction to produce convective hot air.

As with all heating devices, these descriptions are somewhat simplistic. It is conceivable, for instance, that a very efficient and large stove set within the fireplace would provide more heat than a small, inefficient stove set on the hearth just outside the fireplace. That is where the consumer comes in. You must study the brochures and the specifications to see if you are getting the maximum heat you can expect from your unit.

In choosing a fireplace stove, look for high-grade materials; steel is every bit as good as cast iron, but both come in different grades. Be sure it is an airtight model; the dealer has to tell you that it isn't if you ask. Airtight isn't quite what it sounds, but any stove that can be designated airtight is better built, will have a longer burn time, and will be easier to manage efficiently.

If the stove has a viewing window, be sure it is easily removed in the event of breakage; preferably, you should be able to take it out yourself.

If you want—or think you may want at some future date—a wood stove with coal capability, be sure that the stove you are considering will burn anthracite. Many manufacturers say their stoves are dual-fuel stoves, suitable for both coal or wood—but careful reading of their literature sometimes reveals that they mean wood and a low-grade coal, such as lignite. This is by no means equivalent to an anthracite-burning stove. All coal stoves will burn wood; very few wood stoves are suitable for burning coal. More and more wood stove manufacturers are making coal conversion kits available; some work well and some do not. Do not forgo shaker grates, ashpans, and other coal-burning aids unless you are fairly sure you will never want to burn coal.

Ask your dealer about parts replacement. He will have had experience with the manufacturer and will usually tell you if it has been good.

Fireplace Inserts

A fireplace insert is a comparatively recent development. It grew out of homeowners' desire for a device that would increase the efficiency and heat production of their fireplace but that would not require extensive construction, and that they could usually install themselves. Most manufacturers of inserts go to considerable trouble to design their units so that they practically slide into the fireplace, and each step that must be taken in the installation is usually spelled out in great detail. The average homeowner will find it easier to install an insert than to put together a child's bicycle.

Another feature of the inserts is that they generally come complete with any special tools (a masonry bit, etc.) that may be needed, as well as all the necessary screws, bolts, and fiberglass (for a tight seal).

Inserts are usually meant to be installed in an existing masonry fireplace. You need to measure your fireplace (the manufacturer will provide illustrated literature showing you how to do this) to determine which size will fit best. If you have an odd-sized fireplace, many manufacturers will customize a unit for you. Inserts are available to fit about 90 to 95 percent of existing fireplaces, including corner fireplaces and see-through ones. If one manufacturer does not have what you need, keep looking.

As you will see when you glance through Part 4: The Wood- and Coal-burner's Catalog, inserts not only come in a wide range of sizes and trim; they also work in many different ways. It will be much easier to read and absorb the special features of each in Part 4 than to run around to various dealers (no one dealer carries them all). Once you settle on the type you want, familiarize yourself with the variations available as shown herein. If you then encounter a new insert you haven't previously heard of, you will know the features to look for, the questions to ask, and will probably know immediately which unit it is similar to.

Inserts are usually considered for supplemental heat or as backup units to solar heat. It is generally unrealistic to expect an insert to heat your whole house. It can increase the heat production of your fireplace considerably—usually about three times—and will prevent the fireplace flue from drawing heat out of the house while the fire is dying down. The glass doors cut down on the heat radiated directly from the fire—although Corning says its glass actually increases heat production—but the convective heat usually more than makes up for this loss. Adding a blower usually increases hot air production, though there are a few units that are said to produce just as large quantities of hot air without the need of blowers.

Inserts, in general, seem to have attracted the most attention of ingenious designers and engineers. The challenge to create a better insert seems to stimulate a number of people who have used this type of unit, and new ideas are being put into production all the time. Since inserts are not yet subject to labeling, the consumer has to use his own judgment as to which ideas seem soundest. If you can find a satisfied user, you can ask some of the questions that may occur to you.

Many inserts are sold direct from the factory to the consumer; the manufacturers appear to be happy to answer questions and provide all the information a consumer could want. If you are puzzled about how a unit works, don't hesitate to call the manufacturer—who may also be the inventor—and ask about it.

One of the problems with making an intelligent choice among the many inserts available is that this is a comparatively new item. Ordinarily, you can be guided to some extent by a manufacturer's reputation; in this case, some of the devices have just come on the market and do not have a track record. Rely heavily on the reputation of the dealer. He is the one to whom you will complain and he knows it. Ask him his opinion as to quality, and have him show you in what ways he thinks one unit is better than another. After you have done this a couple of times, you will be able to judge many of the features for yourself. If a dealer carries only one unit, ask him why. He will naturally try to sell you on it and you can use these arguments with the next dealer, who is carrying some other line.

Once you have satisfied yourself that several of the units you are considering are comparable in quality, price, options, and heat production, consider appearance. Your fireplace is part of your décor and you will not be happy with one that doesn't fit in. Often units will come in either a matte black finish or brass. Many combine the two, with brass trim optional. Do not assume the unit you see at the dealer's is identical to the one you are ordering; ask if some of the items are optional.

Once the dealer has quoted a price, inquire if that includes installation; get the price before you ask. If it does, find out the cost if you install it yourself. If it doesn't, determine the surcharge for installation. Always ask whether there is a delivery charge.

Built-ins

A built-in is a fireplace that you add where none existed before. There are basically two types—those with a masonry shell and those known as zero clearance. You've probably seen brochures with color photographs of a happy couple installing wood framing around a fireplace and ending up—after a series of photographs—with what looks like a standard fireplace.

Zero Clearance Units

Zero clearance fireplaces are easy to install and much cheaper than a masonry fireplace. You can put them anywhere because they are designed to be set directly on wood floors and to rest right against the wood framing studs that you box them in with. They require no clearance to combustibles, which is why they are called zero clearance. You add a hearth and a certain amount of fireproof material, but it is all very simple and the chimney is usually something like a triple-walled affair that goes up through the floors and attic and roof without the benefit of masonry or firetile. If you don't have a fireplace and you want one, this may be the solution. There are many brands of zero clearance fireplaces and they are all clearly identified and come with detailed instructions. You have to be handy enough to do framing, but that is not highly skilled work; a friendly carpenter might be willing to lend you a hand in the beginning to show you how to measure and cut the studs and how to attach them to the rest of the framing. When installing any fireplace or stovepipe, be sure to take all the safety precautions the manufacturer specifies. If you want to put the fireplace and chimney on an outside wall, you can even box it in with brick facing so that it will look like a masonry chimney. If you feel at all hesitant, have the installation done by a professional.

Masonry Shell

This kind of built-in can run into money because it requires a solid foundation and usually a masonry chimney goes along with it. Not only is this type of construction expensive; it is not for amateurs. You will need a workman who knows how to build chimneys. If all his references are for building stone walls and terraces, look further.

Retrofits

A retrofit is any unit that can be fitted into an existing fireplace. It includes many of the types we have already discussed—all inserts, for instance, can be retrofitted—but it sometimes includes units you wouldn't think could be adapted to this type of installation. Once you know what the word means, you can understand the manufacturer's brochure better. If he says his unit can be retrofitted, and if you have an existing fireplace, you know you can consider buying it.

Grates

I am discussing here the more elaborate types of grate, which use either hot air or water to increase heat production. These are more efficient than the grates you can simply put in your open fireplace instead of andirons.

If it is an air-circulating grate, not only will it provide radiant heat from the log fire (like a standard fireplace); it will also draw in room air through the hollow C-tubes (tubes in the shape of a C, with the logs resting on the bottom curve), heat it, and send it back out into the room over the top of the fire as hot air. The air will circulate by natural convection. Many C-grates can be installed with an optional blower, which will increase air production, but that requires a nearby electrical outlet.

In buying a grate, one of the things to beware of is too thin metal. If the grate or the tubes are constructed of metal of an insufficiently heavy gauge, they will burn out in a very short time. Some grates are so poor that they will not give more than a few months of service. The manufacturer's warranty or guarantee against burn-out is some protection against this happening, as well as an indication of how sturdy the grate is. Since these warranties are usually for less than the probable life of the device, you can use them as a fairly accurate indication of minimum useful life. To some extent, however, the durability of these devices depends on how well you manage the fire; you can shorten the life of any grate by using it improperly.

If you want to go a step further, you can enclose the fireplace and the C-grate behind glass doors (sometimes offered by the manufacturer, sometimes not). This improves your heating situation greatly because you can leave the damper open overnight without draining all the warm air out of the house and up the open chimney flue. Few householders are going to sit around and wait until the fire is completely out and then close the damper. With the glass doors, you just close everything up tight and go to bed.

If you like, you can add a heat exchanger instead of the C-tubes, and if this produces enough hot air, you can even duct it into adjoining rooms.

The Thermograte people supply everything from a simple C-grate all the way up to a large, enclosed unit (still based on the C-grate) which they claim will heat a sizable area. They've been in business a long time and they sell direct to the consumer, so you can ask them about their product if you are interested.

If convected air doesn't intrigue you sufficiently, how about hot-water heating? Most of these units have "hydro" in their names to indicate that they heat water rather than air. This is not a new idea, but it has been developed in the past few years to the point where you can hook up your fireplace to your existing boiler and through it to your present hot-water baseboard heating system. This is particularly interesting as a solar backup system, and it is much cheaper than electricity. A full-fledged system must be installed by a licensed plumber; do-it-yourselfers take note of the "must."

Utilizing Outside Air

All I've been talking about so far are the units that use room air (except for the hot-water systems), but there are a number of units (both retrofits and built-ins) that use outside air.

The question that immediately comes to mind is: How do you get outside air into the fireplace, and the answer is quite simple: By ducting. You must build a duct from the fireplace to an outside wall. If your fireplace happens to be on an outside wall, this is really simple and anyone can do it. If your fireplace is on an inside wall, you may be able to run the duct beneath the floor between the floor joists to reach an outside wall. Since this will probably mean taking up and putting back part of the flooring, you may want to get a carpenter to do it. This will add to the cost but it isn't a complicated job, so don't let him make a big thing of it. Metal ducts that fit together (like stovepipe) are usually available at any building supply center.

Where the air comes into the unit depends on the unit. Some manufacturers believe outside air should be ducted to the fire to be used for combustion. Others scoff at that and say it should be used as convective air. The latter argue that otherwise the room air is recirculated and reheated over and over again and becomes stale and dusty and unhealthful. The other school says enough air always comes in from the outside to keep the house fresh, but that using outside air for combustion makes for a better, more efficient, and hotter fire. I'm not enough of an engineer to decide between the two theories, but you can assess both and decide for yourself. Incidentally, the original Franklin stove, designed by Ben himself, used ducted outside air for both combustion and convective hot air: maybe he had the right idea. We haven't come as far as we sometimes think we have.

Blowers

Heat rises, cool air sinks; this simple principle has been applied to create devices that take in cool room air at floor level, heat it by channeling it around the fire, and venting it out as hot air into the room. Natural convection will produce a steady flow of air, but many units increase the quantity of air thus circulated through the use of electrically operated blowers.

The one advantage of blowers is that they do increase the hot air production of the units they are attached to; sometimes the increase is sufficient to warrant ducting to adjoining rooms, which are then heated by the same fire.

There are, however, some disadvantages to blower-assisted units. The first one—easy to overlook—is noise. Many blower units require that the fans run whenever there is a fire in the unit. The steady, even though low-pitched, sound of the fan can be irritating to someone who minds that sort of thing. That many consumers buy manually defrosting refrigerators and freezers, rather than automatic defrosting units, in order to avoid the continuous noise of the defrosting fan, indicates that noise is a consideration for some people. The ambience of a quiet evening by the fire, watching the flickering flames in a softly lighted room, is not enhanced by the steady roar of the blower. If you can sublimate the sound, thinking of it as sort of a purr, it probably won't bother you a bit; a friend of mine hadn't even noticed the fan sound until I mentioned it. Some manufacturers go out of their way to assert that their blower is especially quiet; take note of this if the feature is important to you.

Another disadvantage is the extra cost. Most manufacturers give some indication of how much it costs to run the fan; the assumption is that the consumer will be pleasantly surprised at how little it costs, and the comparison is usually made to the cost of operating the appropriate light bulb. Whatever it costs, it is an additional and constant expense and you may want to take it into consideration.

Where the blower is positioned may also be a factor. If the blower is behind the unit—between it and the back wall of the firebox—it is subjected to very high heat, which may damage it. Usually, units that should not be operated without the blower in use require that primarily to protect the blower and keep it cooler; it is seldom to protect the unit. If the blower is housed outside the unit, that usually means you have a box sitting on the hearth, on one side or the other of the fireplace opening. Most blower housings are inconspicuous, but they take up some room and are never truly decorative; look carefully at the photographs in the manufacturer's brochure so that you will not be unpleasantly surprised when you uncrate your unit. There are some units that house their blowers in front, below the firebox. Look for this feature if you find it desirable.

All blowers are electrically operated, which means you must have an electric outlet nearby. If you are planning to use the unit in a cabin or beach house that does not have electricity, a blower unit would not be very practical. Nor should you plan to install one in a fireplace distant from an outlet, so that a long extension cord is required. It would be very easy to pull out a plug with a broom or vacuum cleaner, and if you failed to notice it (as is possible if the plug is disconnected but not pulled entirely out of the socket), and if the blower is essential to the operation of the unit, you might do some permanent damage. There is also the problem of power outages. If the unit cannot be operated without the blower, you would be without its heat just at the time when you need it most. If the power failure occurs when you are away from home, the unit may be damaged before you have a chance to put out the fire.

Blowers are common accessories with fireplace units and can be very helpful in increasing production, so I do not mean to imply that their disadvantages outweigh their advantages. It is important, however, to be aware of all aspects of their use and to ask about noise, operating the unit without a blower, etc., when considering your choice of unit.

Warranties

Always look in the manufacturer's brochure or ask the dealer for a copy of the warranty on a unit you are considering purchasing. A comparatively long, and not too limited, warranty is an indication of the manufacturer's confidence in his product. Read it carefully and be sure you understand what is and what is not covered.

Types of Units

Compare warranties for the same type of unit. The average life of different types of units—an insert, a built-in, or a freestanding stove—is not necessarily the same. If you look at the warranties for three or four different brands of the same type, you will get an idea of what can be expected in terms of the life of the unit. The warranty will not usually be for as long a period as the average life of that type of unit, but it will *indicate* the optimum years of use you can reasonably expect.

Wood- and coal-burning units, more than most other household appliances, can have their lives shortened considerably by abuse. A homeowner who regularly builds too hot a fire, overloads the firebox, or ignores the manufacturer's instructions for managing the fire is asking for trouble; it is not reasonable to expect the manufacturer to undertake to back up his product under such circumstances. It is possible, therefore, that claims will be looked upon with a jaundiced eye; the manufacturer knows from experience that the consumer is not likely to admit to having done anything incorrectly. Unfortunately for both parties, it is sometimes impossible to determine, for instance, that an insert was operated without the blower when the instructions clearly stated that it should never be operated under those conditions.

Many warranties state specifically that they cover only factory-related defects or defects in workmanship. This, too, is sometimes subject to interpretation. Burn-out, for example, may be due to poor materials and construction, but it is often due to mismanagement of the fire or some other consumer-related problem. The consumer should be realistic enough to understand that an inexpensive grate or C-tube cannot be expected to last as long as an expensive one; the materials will be less heat-resistant, thinner, and more casually constructed. The less expensive item will still be a good buy for the person who wants to try out that type of heat before making a commitment to a more expensive unit. It may be, also, that the unit is required for occasional use—a summer cabin, a ski lodge—and need not be as durable as one in a standard home situation. There is the possibility, too, that cash is short and the less expensive unit is better than nothing at all—with the hope that it may result in savings that will make it possible for you to trade up to a more expensive unit in the future.

In wood- and coal-burning units, price alone is no criterion of quality. There are many other ways to judge a unit, and the length and coverage of the warranty is one of them; the more expensive the unit, the more the manufacturer ought to be willing to back it up.

You will learn, by comparison of warranties, that almost no one will extend any warranty to the glass used in glass doors. Although there is a range in the quality and heat resistance of the glass used—some seem to stand up better than others—even the best glass will break on occasion. There are exceptions to this; a few manufacturers provide a one-year warranty against breakage, confident that the construction of their unit will minimize this problem.

Industry Approvals:
What They Are and What They Mean

The market for wood- and coal-burning devices has grown like Topsy and caught the regulatory commissions by surprise. The result is something of a mess as far as standards are concerned.

In the beginning, consumers were buying just about any wood stoves they could get their hands on, and either doing the installations themselves or hiring any local handyman who would agree to do it for them. Fortunately, local building inspectors quickly realized that this was a potentially dangerous situation and began to require permits before stoves could be installed legally. Unfortunately, most inspectors didn't know any more about wood stove safety or construction than did anyone else; rules and standards were imposed arbitrarily and often were so unreasonable that they encouraged noncompliance.

Another situation that arose was that some states rushed to set up standards and requirements that were accepted statewide but were not, necessarily, recognized by any other state. Massachusetts and Connecticut, for example, made their own rules and weren't the least bit interested in whether or not the manufacturer had gained approvals in other states. This made it difficult for the manufacturer who was trying to get his product on the market as quickly as possible in order to get his share of this new business, and who didn't have the time—let alone the budget—to submit his product for testing to a dozen different labs. In addition, the labs themselves became overwhelmed with the number of units submitted for testing and began to run behind, with the result that a manufacturer waiting for approval could lose the sales of a whole season.

Furthermore, local building inspectors, worried about wood stove safety and aware of their own inability to make judgments in this area, often set standards that made sense for one type of unit or installation but not for another—and to hedge their bets, they tended to be overcautious. In many cases, they even refused to accept the state's standards and insisted on adding some of their own requirements to already adequate or even stringent regulations.

Luckily, a great deal of the panic has subsided as the authorities have come to realize that a wood- or coal-burning stove is not a mysterious and dangerous monster but merely another heating device—no more dangerous than an oil furnace or a gas furnace when properly installed and maintained. Most inspectors, however, require industry approval and are not always in agreement as to which units they will accept. This is difficult, for example, for foreign stove manufacturers, who usually have DIN approval, from a German regulatory agency, which is very stringent and requires, among other things, that stoves be constructed with much closer clearance-to-combustibles ratings than are required of American stoves. DIN approval should be acceptable to inspectors, but many of them, ignorant of its significance, may refuse to honor it. This means the foreign manufacturer must delay his entry into the U.S. market for several months, or even longer, while he is awaiting UL or some similar approval, which may not be nearly so difficult to get as DIN but is more acceptable to local and state authorities. This, in turn, adds to a further overload on American labs and slows up testing and acceptance of American-made stoves.

The proliferation of testing labs and the resulting confusion has led the manufacturers to ask the government to help them arrive at industrywide standards based on a uniform code that would be accepted nationally, rather than on a state-by-state basis. The result of such a program would be a nationally recognized label that would certify the product to be safe when installed according to certain specific requirements. At present, the Consumer Products Safety Commission is in the process of trying to develop rules regulating the installation and maintenance of wood- and coal-burning stoves. The resulting label would include information as to the minimum clearance to combustibles, and the type of chimney acceptable for the installation, and would be required to be prominently affixed to the product. The determination of this information would not be the manufacturer's word or opinion, but would have to be verified through testing, presumably by an independent laboratory. Massachusetts, for example, requires not only this information but also the name of the testing lab and the standard for which the approval was given.

Until such a label is available, you can save yourself a great deal of time and trouble by buying units that have been approved or listed by a model building code authority—ICBO, BOCA, or SBCCI—or by UL. Most building inspectors will accept these approvals because they mean that the unit has satisfactory installation instructions, clearly states minimum clearance to combustibles, has been tested and approved by an independent laboratory, and has been manufactured under a third-party quality-control program that includes periodic inspections of the plant and the product. CSA (the Canadian Standards Association), WEI (the Wood Energy Institute), the Arnold Greene Testing Laboratories, and many other labels may also be acceptable, but you should check your local building inspector before making your purchase. Usually the state will accept any approval or listing by an accredited laboratory, yet state acceptance does not automatically guarantee local inspector acceptance (though you can use the state acceptance as an argument in your favor and it may carry weight).

The Massachusetts System could serve as a model for nationwide labeling. It is the only state with written requirements that clearly set forth the criteria for acceptance. With this in hand, a specific code or laboratory can see what they must provide for acceptance and can conform. This would create a uniform code and would eliminate the uncertainty and chaos that presently exist.

The independent testing laboratories would be happy with a uniform code, providing it was accepted nationwide and did not require them to apply to each state individually, a procedure that would not only be time-consuming but would be prohibitive in cost. The Underwriters Laboratories (UL), whose approval is generally routinely required and accepted on electrical appliances, already do stove testing and could possibly expand their services to provide a national label. This would seem unfair, however, to the many testing labs already set up in various states, with a financial commitment in plant and equipment as well as a going business in stove testing. A fairer solution would certainly seem to be that any lab operating under national regulations and conforming to testing requirements could be authorized to issue a nationally accepted label.

The industry is very aware of the problem and the American Society for Testing and Material (ASTM), the National Bureau of Standards (NBS), and the American Council of Independent Laboratories (ACIL) are all working to develop a uniform code.

As always, the industry is uneasy about the possibility of federal regulation and would prefer industry control of this crucial area. Presently, it is a bit of a race to see who gets off the ground first with a workable national code; the consumer is bound to benefit either way.

Your fireplace stove or device may or may not bear a label attesting to the fact that it is "UL Listed" or "UL Approved" or has some other type of approval.

At present, units that are fireplace inserts do not have any approvals; so far no labels are issued for these devices. This may change in the near future, so always ask.

Most other equipment, including stovepipe, has some sort of listing, approval, or rating. Rather than try to understand exactly what a specific rating means (even UL differentiates between "listing" and "approved," and the test report goes into great detail), take this information with you when you go for your wood stove permit. Some inspectors require that you bring two copies of the manufacturer's sales brochure with you, but do not count on its containing all the pertinent information.

If, on looking over the brochure, you find that it does not mention any approvals or listings, ask the dealer. The growth in state and local requirements for this kind of information caught manufacturers by surprise; they may not have got through the testing labs in time to put the results in the brochure, but they may have received the approval subsequently. Even at the time of writing this book, many manufacturers were still waiting for the test results, and even though they know their stoves are carefully constructed and will be accepted, they have to wait until it is official. Additionally, in order to be scrupulously honest, many of them have temporarily withdrawn claims as to BTU's, etc., until this can be confirmed by independent testing. Even when they know, because of careful testing they have done on their own, that their claims are valid, they often will no longer say so until the figures have been confirmed by an independent laboratory.

While it is all very well to want to be an informed consumer (that is partly the purpose of this book), this is an area in which you would have to be a heating engineer with extensive experience in the field to make any sense of all the possible labels and approvals and listings with which you will be confronted. Since the building or fire inspector exists to ensure the safety of your device and installation, and since he is gradually becoming more knowledgeable, and since you cannot install the unit anyhow unless he approves—no matter what the manufacturer says—I would recommend that you leave it to him. In other words, if you can get a permit, let it go at that.

I think it's more important for you to know how to run the stove or insert, because no one will be looking over your shoulder to check out that you do it right. And you ought to watch when it is being installed (assuming you're not doing it yourself) so that you can answer questions about it if, when the inspector comes to look, the fireplace opening has already been sealed off and cannot really be inspected. You should know, for instance, whether the stove has been vented directly into the fireplace opening or whether it is connected to stovepipe that goes up the flue—and you should know how far up. Ask questions, make notes, and you will make it easier for the inspector to make an intelligent assessment of the safety of your installation. Remember that industry approvals apply to construction materials; how the units are installed is something else entirely.

13

Installation:
No Place for Shortcuts

There are three areas where a wood- or coal-burning homeowner can run into trouble: buying a poor-quality unit; installing it improperly; managing the fire inexpertly. Of the three, the most common cause of house fires is improper installation.

Proper installation begins with where you are going to place and to vent your unit. With fireplace stoves, inserts, and built-ins, this is greatly simplified; they are all placed either on the hearth or within the fireplace—one that already exists or one that you build expressly for the unit you have chosen —and they are vented through the fireplace flue or through a prefab chimney (in the case of the built-in). The hearth presents no problem; you need only determine that its noncombustible surface is large enough to meet the local building code requirements as to how much of it you need in front of the unit you have chosen. If your hearth is too narrow, there are a wide variety of suitable stove boards, both plain and decorative, you can buy. You should, of course, never place any sort of unit directly on a wood floor.

The Chimney

With the types of units we are discussing in this book, the chimney is the most likely source of trouble—trouble, however, that is easily avoided. One must only make sure that the chimney is sound and clean. Assuming it has been properly constructed in the first place, without excessive setbacks or angles, it is only necessary to get it inspected by someone who knows what he is doing. Unfortunately, there are many people who have set themselves up in the business of installing stoves who have no qualifications for this work. I have seen installations that violated the most elementary rules of safety.

One of the most important safety rules is to be certain that your unit is venting into a flue that does not serve any other heating appliance. The most common mistake made is venting a stove into the flue that serves the oil burner in the basement. This is extremely dangerous and should never be done under any circumstances. Chances are, if your house was built with a fireplace, the fireplace has its own flue. If you are installing a built-in, you will also put in a prefab chimney, so that, also, presents no problem. I mention the possibility primarily to make the point that you should be careful to use experienced workmen. Your best bet is to ask for references. If they have installed other units in your area, and if these units have passed inspection, they probably know what they are doing.

CHIMNEY CHECKLIST

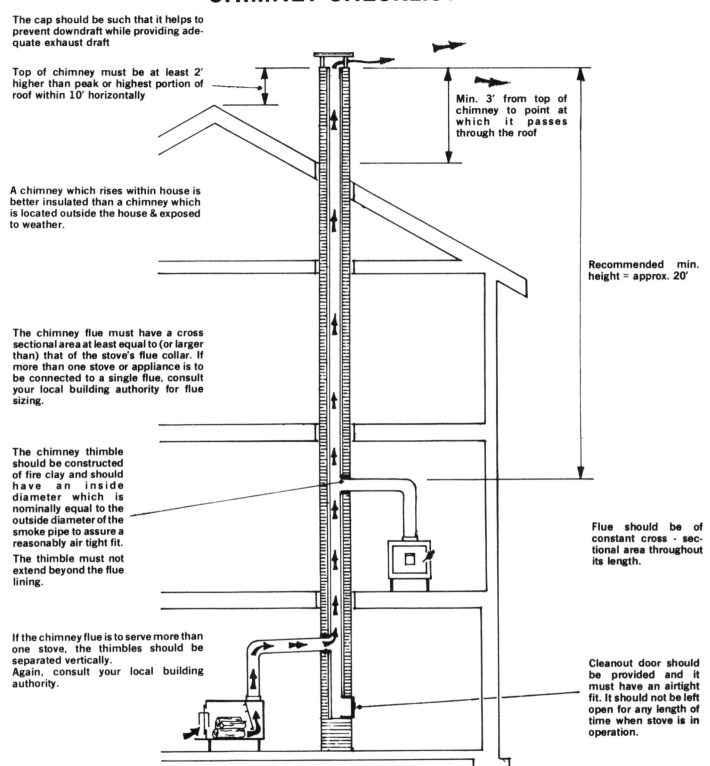

The cap should be such that it helps to prevent downdraft while providing adequate exhaust draft

Top of chimney must be at least 2' higher than peak or highest portion of roof within 10' horizontally

A chimney which rises within house is better insulated than a chimney which is located outside the house & exposed to weather.

The chimney flue must have a cross sectional area at least equal to (or larger than) that of the stove's flue collar. If more than one stove or appliance is to be connected to a single flue, consult your local building authority for flue sizing.

The chimney thimble should be constructed of fire clay and should have an inside diameter which is nominally equal to the outside diameter of the smoke pipe to assure a reasonably air tight fit.

The thimble must not extend beyond the flue lining.

If the chimney flue is to serve more than one stove, the thimbles should be separated vertically.
Again, consult your local building authority.

Min. 3' from top of chimney to point at which it passes through the roof

Recommended min. height = approx. 20'

Flue should be of constant cross - sectional area throughout its length.

Cleanout door should be provided and it must have an airtight fit. It should not be left open for any length of time when stove is in operation.

Page from National Stove Works' Thermo-Control Owner's Manual and Wood Burning Handbook, showing the thoroughness with which the manufacturer covers important safety rules.

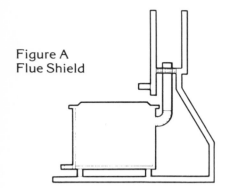

Figure A
Flue Shield

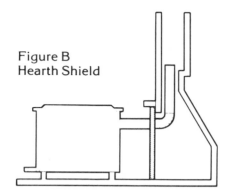

Figure B
Hearth Shield

Two ways of closing off chimney. Figure A shows flue shield closing opening at throat of chimney. Figure B shows fireplace closure shield.
COURTESY HEATHDELLE SALES ASSOCIATES, INC.

The next thing to check is whether the chimney leaks. The flue lining of a masonry chimney may deteriorate over the years and may crack. Sometimes the cracks are so extensive that it is possible to go into an upstairs room or an attic and see smoke coming into the room from the juncture of baseboard and wall. A fire in the fireplace may also cause an upstairs wall to feel warm to the touch. It is not, however, necessary to test the flue lining in these ways since it can be inspected visually with a flashlight and a mirror. If your house is old, the chimney may have been built without a flue lining, in which case you may be able to see the stone or brick, of which the chimney proper is constructed, from inside the flue. A chimney without a flue lining will deteriorate faster than one that is lined. If you have an old, unlined chimney, consider adding a liner. Vitrified clay linings, both round and rectangular, are available; prefab pipe can sometimes be used instead, if you prefer.

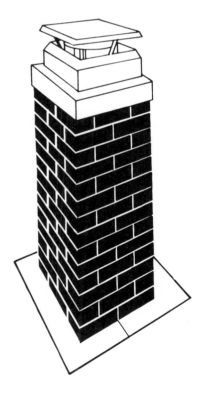

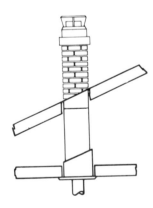

Prefab chimney assembly, including: rain cap assembly; two slip joints; decorative housing; flashing; two straps.
COURTESY PREWAY

In addition to the lining, be sure the part of the chimney that extends above the roof is checked. The bricks or stone may need pointing or the protective mortar layer along the top may need to be replaced. In some areas, builders pay extra to use old brick—because of its lovely mellow color—and most homeowners consider this a plus. But old brick may deteriorate much faster than you might expect, and a chimney of old brick may need to be taken down and replaced after as little as twelve or fifteen years.

Be sure that any prefabricated chimney you use either is UL tested and approved or has an equivalent label.

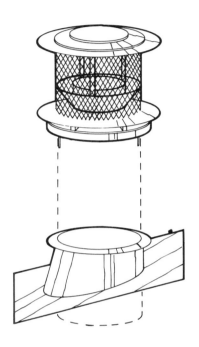 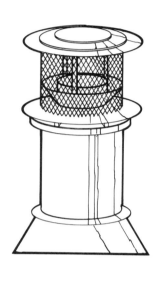 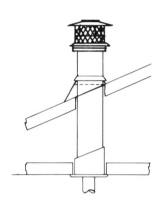

Prefab chimney assembly, including: flashing; adapter; storm collar; rain cap; rain shield; and spark arrester. Pipe not included. COURTESY PREWAY

There are different grades of prefab chimneys for different fuels. Since you may start out with wood and then decide to switch to coal, it is best to get the kind that is listed "for all fuels." You can then rest assured that it will withstand even the very hottest fires your unit can handle.

Flue pipe, or chimney pipe, comes a number of different ways. It can be insulated, double walled, triple walled, and so on. The siphoning types cool the inner pipe, through which the volatiles pass, with moving air, drawn down and then channeled up to the outside again. There is considerable difference of opinion regarding this type of pipe. Many experts swear by it, but others claim that it accelerates the deposit of creosote because it keeps the stack temperatures cooler than would otherwise be the case. You will probably have to take the advice of the person doing the work, but it wouldn't hurt to get a contrary opinion and decide for yourself which sounds better to you.

If you are installing a built-in, the manufacturer will furnish a certain amount of the type of flue pipe he recommends and will supply more of it as an option, if necessary. The prefab chimney helps keep the built-in lightweight (compared to a masonry fireplace and chimney) and eliminates the need for extensive footing, usually to ground level. If you want a prefab chimney to look like a masonry chimney, for appearance' sake, you can add brick or stone facing, imitation or real.

If your chimney doesn't draw well because the flue is too large, a prefab chimney inside it might be an inexpensive way to correct the problem.

Inspecting and repairing a masonry chimney is no job for an amateur; don't plan to make it a do-it-yourself project. On the other hand, installing a built-in and a prefab chimney is well within the capability of a handy homeowner.

NOTE: DO NOT CONFUSE SINGLE WALL STOVEPIPE WITH PREFAB CHIMNEY PIPE. AS THE ASHLEY MANUAL FLATLY STATES: "A SINGLE WALL METAL CHIMNEY MUST NOT BE USED WITH THIS OR ANY OTHER WOOD HEATER."

Stovepipe

If you need stovepipe—as in installing a fireplace stove—you must take care that it is of sufficient thickness to be safe. What you need to know is the gauge of the pipe. The lower the number—18 gauge, 14 gauge, 12 gauge, etc.—the thicker the metal. Check your local building code for the gauge of stovepipe your town requires.

Don't try to get away with installing a thinner gauge than is required; you would risk a house fire. (With too thin a pipe there is danger of burning right through the metal.)

I've had many people ask me which way to install the pipe. Since it comes in sections, you have the option of putting the crimped ends down toward the stove or up toward the chimney. It is generally recommended that the crimped ends be toward the stove. Thus, any melting creosote will run harmlessly down into the stove. If the pipe sections are installed the other way, the creosote is liable to drip on the floor. Sometimes, also, special wind conditions will cause a small amount of rain to come down the chimney. If it runs into the stove, you won't even know it, but if the pipe were fitted the other way, it might drip outside the joinings and make a smelly mess on the hearth.

Do-It-Yourself Installations

Only you know how good a handyman you are. In installing heating units, however, it is important to underestimate your skills; you are dealing with fire and mistakes can be costly in terms of property, and possibly your life. One installation almost anyone can do safely, providing a professional inspection of chimney and fireplace has been made, is of inserts.

Inserts. Inserts are designed to be installed by any homeowner who knows how to use a few simple tools, such as a screwdriver. The manufacturer will provide step-by-step instructions, clearly illustrated with line drawings, to show you what you should be doing at each stage. If any tool is required that a homeowner might not normally have in the family tool chest, it is furnished by the manufacturer.

As long as you can read and follow simple instructions, you will find installing an insert no problem at all.

There is only one area in which you will need help. Look at the shipping weight of the insert in the specifications given in Part Four. Many of these weights include the crate; many of them do not. You will see that they weigh a couple of hundred pounds, on the average, and it doesn't take much imagination to realize that it is going to take more than one person to manhandle the

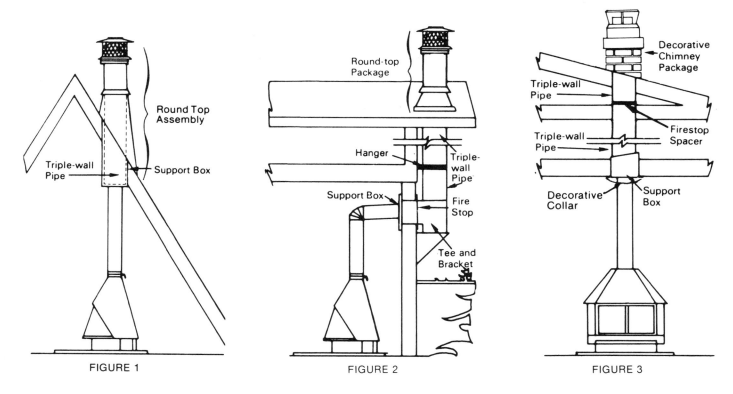

FIGURE 1

FIGURE 2

FIGURE 3

Prefab installations, showing: (1) A-frame roof; (2) elbowing through outside wall to avoid attic; (3) running pipe through closet or box; (4) elbow to clear upstairs obstacles; (5) chase-top installation; (6) mobile or modular home installation. COURTESY PREWAY

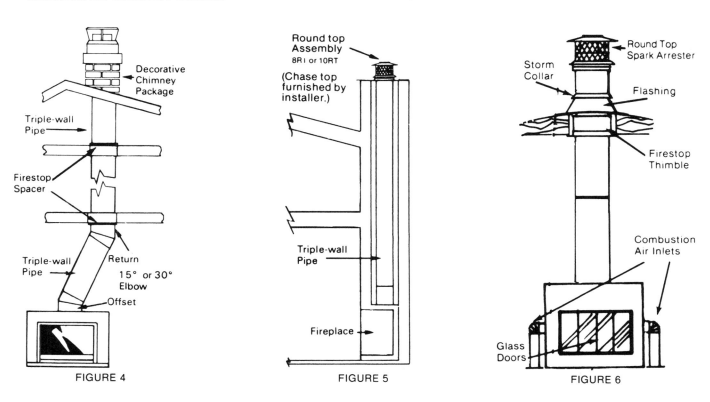

FIGURE 4

FIGURE 5

FIGURE 6

unit into place. The instructions usually read something like this, at a certain point: "Slide unit into fireplace opening." That sounds easy, but the unit is bulky and awkward and it isn't on wheels; sliding it into place is less simple than it sounds, unless you have two husky men doing it. It is true that there is a knack to moving heavy objects, and I have seen heavy steel stoves, made even heavier by a full firebrick lining in place, maneuvered into position by a single elderly—but experienced—man. Anyone who has been moved knows that moving men have tricks all their own and can single-handedly manage pieces of furniture the average householder can hardly budge. Unless you are experienced in moving heavy objects, I think you will need help at this point. Since the unit will have to be removed each season by whoever cleans the chimney, and also for maintenance, you might want to buy a dolly to make the job easier.

Built-ins. A built-in requires framing and other construction. Manufacturers' brochures usually show a happy couple doing all this themselves, so I guess it is possible. I would not recommend it, however, unless you can really see yourself carrying out the procedures shown in these pictures. If you do, follow the instructions to the letter (and check them ahead of time with your building inspector).

Fireplace stoves. Installing a stove that is to be vented into a fireplace flue is really very easy, except for the weight of the stove. Chimney sweeps can usually manage to move stoves single-handedly, but they don't enjoy that part of their work. Connecting the stovepipe, even bolting the sections together, is no big deal. Get whoever delivers the stove to show you how to tilt it for easier handling and how to work it into position. If it is too heavy for you, two untrained but husky high school students can easily manage. Be sure you know how far the stovepipe should extend up the flue, how to disengage the flue damper, and the proper pitch for the pipe as it leaves the vent on the back of the stove. Follow instructions, also, for sealing the fireplace opening, or the flue opening if you use the Tempwood Damper Panel kit (see Part Four).

Clearance to Combustibles

"Clearance to combustibles" is a phrase you will encounter over and over in brochures, articles, installation instructions, and other literature relating to wood- and coal-burning equipment. In some ways, it is the single most important fact you need to know about the unit you purchase.

Combustibles are any objects capable of burning, including wood, upholstery, paper, clothing, cardboard, and the fur on the family cat. The cat will move away if he gets too hot, but the other objects depend on you to keep them at a safe distance. Clearance to combustibles tells you how far away the combustible object must be in order not to catch fire from the heat source; it is usually expressed in terms of inches, as in "Clearance to combustibles 36" or "Zero clearance to combustibles," meaning no clearance required.

All coal- and wood-burning equipment manufacturers must state, in their installation instructions, what the clearance to combustibles is for their product. A large mail order house was recently ordered to recall, or pay for correcting the installation of, hundreds of thousands of their stoves, not because the stoves were not well constructed, but because the installation instructions were not sufficiently clear and detailed. Lacking adequate instructions, the purchaser might have installed the unit improperly, due to ignorance of the proper procedure, thus rendering the installation—hence the stove itself—unsafe.

Before you buy a unit, determine how close it will come to combustibles and whether it will be possible to install safely. If you don't check this out, you may get the unit installed, only to have the building inspector refuse to issue you a permit (because clearance to combustibles is one of the first things he will check). In most instances, 36 inches is the minimum clearance to combustibles required, but you cannot be sure unless you read the manufacturer's manual. The manual for one wood-burning stove on the market states clearly: "The minimum clearance between the stove, top, sides or rear and any unprotected combustible surface or material is 48 inches." Do not take clearances for granted; check them out.

If you bring a drawing (it can be very rough) of your fireplace, indicating all nearby wood—the mantel, the facing on the sides and top, any paneling—the dealer can help you check the unit you are considering. You can't do this before you have decided which stove or insert you are purchasing, because the dimensions of the various stoves differ, and that will affect your calculations.

Do not forget to indicate the width and length of your hearth—the fireproof area of brick, slate, etc., outside your fireplace opening. If it is insufficient, you may need to purchase a noncombustible mat to protect the wood floor or carpeting beyond the hearth. Fireproof mats are available from stove manufacturers (they will be listed among their accessories), stove dealers, and home centers. You can get very plain, simple brown ones or handsome decorative panels in a variety of colors and patterns.

If you need to protect a wood mantel, you will find that many manufacturers offer a heat shield as an accessory to their stoves or inserts; some include them with the stove at no extra charge. Check the size of the shield (ask for the dimensions) against your requirements. They are sometimes a little skimpy, and this is no area in which to be penny wise. Do not, however, assume that the mantel is all you need to protect. No manufacturer seems to worry about the wood between the top of the fireplace opening and the mantel or on the sides of the fireplace, in spite of the fact that this is a common way of facing a fireplace. *They* may not worry about it but you have to, so include all these features in your drawing.

The next step is to look at the installation instructions. You will find that clearances to combustibles vary according to what part of the stove you are considering. The bottom of the stove, for instance, does not usually produce very much heat. If it does, the legs are usually high enough to make it safe when placed on a suitable mat (never place a stove directly on a wood floor). Stoves that burn coal can usually be placed closer to the floor because the required grate, plus the ashpan between the firebox and the bottom of the stove, all serve to reduce the amount of heat radiated from the bottom. Unfortunately, I have known some building inspectors to refuse to accept that fact and to require the same clearance for a stove with a bottom ashpan as for a cast-iron box stove with nothing between the firebox and the floor except the bottom plate. In one case, the dealer offered to demonstrate with a thermometer that the heat beneath the stove never reached unacceptable levels, but the inspector was adamant. Since the height of the legs of this particular model was lower than those of stoves generally, it came too close for even a noncombustible mat installation and the inspector's position effectively barred the sale of an excellent and a very popular stove—as well as an eminently safe one—in his area. His stubbornness was not due to any personal prejudice but simply to the fact that he was ignorant of the nature of wood- and coal-burning stoves and was not going to take any chances. He followed the most extreme clearance to combustibles requirements without allowing for instances where lesser distances were safe and proper. As these units become more common, inspectors are becoming more knowledgeable, and you will encounter this situation less and less; a nationwide standard of labeling will also solve the problem, because the labels will clearly state the distance to combustibles accepted as safe for each stove. In the meantime, however, be sure to check your choice and your installation with your local building inspector before you make any purchase.

If you have a reasonable and experienced inspector, you may be able to choose a stove that, because of the nature of its construction can be set quite close to combustibles. Any stove bearing the German DIN industry approval, for instance, can be set closer to combustibles than 36 inches because that is one of the requirements for approval. Most of the time, this closer clearance is achieved through an air space between the firebox and the outside of the unit. The outside becomes a shell—as in the Weso tile stove—and with the air space between it and the firebox, never becomes as hot as the outside of the firebox. A typical Scandinavian cast-iron stove, on the other hand, requires the maximum clearances because the firebox is the stove.

Even in the case of maximum clearances, however, you will find that front, back, sides, top, and bottom have different requirements; the manufacturer's instructions will give them all—usually in the form of a drawing with the clearances clearly indicated.

Even if you have installed your unit safely, you have to keep a sharp eye out to make sure that violations do not creep in. Your mantel and other fixed objects are no problem; once you have determined they are safe, they will not move. Chairs, couches, footstools, the Sunday paper, are all, however, liable to be moved or left too close to the fire. The family should be instructed as to safe distances and everyone should realize that a house fire can result from carelessness in this area. Wood brought in for the fire should be stored just as far away as any other wood—even if it is wet or icy and therefore temporarily safe. Wet wood can dry out faster than you might expect and you are better off not allowing any exceptions to the clearance to combustibles rule.

Some people tend to think the clearances required are excessive and prove it by putting their hand on a mantel over a stove that has been running a good fire for several hours. "See," one man told me, "it's barely warm. That would never catch on fire." I explained that you cannot judge the likelihood of combustion in that fashion because you are dealing with more than the problem of immediate temperatures. The constant "warming" of the wood dries it out increasingly and imperceptibly until it eventually reaches the stage of being subject to almost spontaneous combustion. At this point it takes very little to cause it to catch fire and that is how most mantel fires occur. Take the clearances to combustibles seriously and do not deviate from them by so much as an inch.

For the types of stoves we are discussing in this book—fireplace stoves set directly against the fireplace opening, inserts, built-ins, and zero clearance fireplaces—we are not dealing with lengths of stovepipe outside the fireplace proper. I would like to mention, however, that if you are installing a stove that has a length of stovepipe between the stove and the fireplace opening, you have to take into account the clearance to combustibles rating from the pipe to any nearby combustibles. Stovepipe gets very hot (unless it is triple-walled, and that is not the type you would be using at that point in your installation) and must always be considered in this connection.

Study the brochures and installation instructions carefully. Many inserts do not sit entirely within the fireplace but extend two or more inches outside of it. The manufacturer will recommend a heat shield "for a low mantel" if his unit requires it, and that is a clue to you to check out the clearances. Do not assume an insert does not require a heat shield.

Another clue is whether a unit must be installed "only in a masonry fireplace." Zero clearance fireplaces do not require the same care—that's why they are named "zero clearance."

Venting Directly into the Fireplace

To make it easier for the homeowner to install them, many fireplace stoves come with a closure panel that can be made to seal off the opening completely (by adding fiberglass or a similar material wherever the panel edges don't fit tightly). Others lack this panel, which the homeowner must then buy from the dealer or a local supplier of this type of equipment. In both instances, however, the installation instructions often say to bring the stove vent up to the opening in the panel (cut to vent size, such as 6 or 8 inches) and, making sure it is a tight fit, consider the installation complete.

What this means, of course, is that the stove is first venting into the fireplace proper, and only eventually finding its way up the chimney by means of the draft. I have spoken at conventions of chimney sweeps, and there invariably arises the question of how to deal with a fireplace that has this type of installation. It seems that after a while the creosote build-up becomes a hard, shiny black surface throughout the inside of the fireplace; the problem is how to remove it when cleaning and sweeping. I usually direct this question to the audience and so far not a single chimney sweep has found a way to get the black stuff off fireplace walls. They usually go ahead and clean the chimney, sweep away any soot, and simply close the whole thing up again, telling the homeowner that is the best that can be done. Should the homeowner ever want to use the fireplace again, or remove the unit (when selling the house, for instance), this unsightly surface could be a disadvantage.

There is also the question of whether this system increases creosote build-up in the chimney. As long as the escaping volatiles are hot, they will not leave deposits on the chimney; it is only as they cool that they precipitate. I would think that vented directly into the fireplace, the volatiles would be cooler by the time they hit the chimney flue than if they were vented into the chimney. If this is true, it could mean the chimney would require cleaning much oftener than is otherwise necessary (usually, cleaning once a year is considered sufficient, if you are burning dry hardwood in a properly managed fire).

In addition, if creosote and soot build-up on the inside of the chimney causes chimney fires (and this is still a matter of argument, although chimney fires do occur somehow), I should think creosote and soot build-up on the inside of the fireplace would cause a fireplace fire (and we know this does happen). I would think, also, that in this case fireplace fires would be more common than chimney fires, since sparks have less distance to travel and might easily ignite something flammable in the fireplace, whereas the additional distance they have to travel to the chimney would cause many of them to go out.

I asked some of the stove manufacturers who recommended in-fireplace venting about the problems and they said the draft was so good at that point that the volatiles would be drawn up the chimney and not have time to deposit on the fireplace walls, and also that at that stage, the volatiles were so hot that they wouldn't be in the precipitating stage. Since the chimney sweeps report that, on the contrary, there is creosote and soot build-up, I don't feel these theories check out, and I strongly advise against venting directly into the fireplace—even if your building inspector will allow it (and he probably won't).

What I recommend instead is installing stovepipe and an elbow to vent into the fireplace flue—in other words, up the chimney. I have had installers recommend extending the pipe *all the way* up the chimney in order to avoid any creosote build-up within the chimney itself. If the chimney is in poor repair and unsafe to use, I suppose you could do this, provided you used triple-wall or equivalent pipe as a replacement for the chimney. Otherwise, I cannot see the point of it, because while creosote would definitely be prevented from forming on the inside of the chimney, it would simply form on the inside of the pipe instead. So at the end of the season you would have to clean the pipe anyway (instead of the chimney).

There is no doubt that it is more trouble to install a fireplace stove with pipe and elbow rather than merely fit it to the vent opening in the closure panel, and this seems to be why the manufacturer argues against it. Most people buying these stoves apparently want one they can install themselves and the easier it is, the better. Actually, however, it is not that much more difficult, as long as you take note of the weight of the stove and hire a couple of sturdy fellows to help you hoist it into place when you are ready. It's not a one-person job even done the "easy" way, unless you're handy with heavy objects and know how to manage them. Look at the weight of the unit you are considering before you assume you can manage it by yourself.

Humidity: A Key to Comfort

One of the problems with domestic heating is that the heating process tends to dry out the air. Air that is too dry is not healthful—for your lungs, your skin, or your furniture. Dry air means more dust, and deterioration of books, wood fibers, and other household items. In addition, too low humidity may make you feel chilly even though the temperature may be almost 70 degrees F.

If this is the case, you may wonder why people say "It's not the heat, it's the humidity." The reason is that warm air can hold more moisture than cold air, so it becomes saturated with much more moisture. (On the other hand, excess humidity can make a cold day feel colder.) It's almost impossible to make a winter house heated by man-made devices *too* humid. The problem usually is how to create a healthful humidity level in this usually arid environment.

If you want to know whether your house is too dry in the winter, here are a few indications. Do you wake up in the morning with your nose and throat passages feeling dry? Does walking across a carpet generate static electricity? (You can tell if you get a shock when you touch metal or another person after doing so.)

Even without these indicators, you can almost assume that a heated house is too dry. Here's a simple test to check it out. Put three ice cubes in a glass and fill it with cold water. Let it stand for three minutes. If by then the outside of the glass has begun to sweat, the humidity level is acceptable.

If the humidity is too low, take steps to remedy the situation. The most effective way is to buy a humidifier. Humidifiers come in all prices and sizes. The best are fairly large—about the size of a night table—but are usually able to be wheeled from room to room, as needed. Predictably, they are also the most expensive, but you can get a good discount by waiting for a sale. Smaller ones—similar to those used in children's rooms and in hospitals—are less expensive but are also effective in a much smaller area. When you first use a humidifier, put a large piece of plastic on the floor under it; sometimes the adjustment or the direction of the mist is such that it makes the floor damp. This is not only not where you need the moisture; it will ruin a wood floor or cause problems with carpeting.

The cheapest device is a pan of water placed in the room. If you have a fireplace stove with enough flat surface, you can put the pan directly on that surface. Be sure the water container is metal (stainless steel or enamel is best because neither will rust) so that the heat of the stove will accelerate evaporation of the water. The first time you do this, you will be amazed at how fast the water evaporates; you will also be pleasantly surprised at how much more comfortable you feel. If you have a zero clearance fireplace or another unit that doesn't have sufficient extension beyond the fireplace opening to provide this surface, you may be able to place a narrow container inside the heated air outlet (usually it is covered with a screen or similar device). If this cannot be done, placing the pan near a fan (or the unit's blower) will accelerate evaporation.

14

A Maintenance Manual

A homeowner soon becomes resigned to the fact that everything about a house, from the washing machine to the roof, requires a certain amount of maintenance. Fuel oil companies offer annual oil burner service contracts which include regular maintenance, as well as repairs and parts replacement. Fireplace stoves, inserts, and built-ins also require maintenance if they are to continue to work efficiently and safely. In this case, however, there is no service contract; the homeowner must assume the responsibility of keeping his unit and its installation in good working order.

Your owner's manual should give you specific instructions regarding maintenance of their particular unit. Sometimes maintenance suggestions are more or less buried in the installation instructions; in that case, note them with a colored pen, for easy reference, or put them on a file card where you can be sure to find them at the end of the season.

Maintaining the Chimney

You have, I hope, inspected the chimney before installing your unit. If it was in good repair at that time, annual cleaning and visual inspection should give you ample warning of any work that needs to be done. Sweeping a chimney is not difficult, unless yours requires that you climb onto the attic roof of a two-story colonial; you can purchase a chimney sweep kit or hire a chimney sweep. Be sure all stovepipe and the interior of the stove itself is examined and cleaned at the same time.

Maintaining Your Unit

Built-ins

A built-in cannot be pulled out, so you must examine it from inside the firebox. Look for rust, test for thin spots; try to notice anything that looks different from the way it looked when it was first built (except that it may have become discolored by heat). Be sure all door latches, draft controls, and vents are clean and free from dirt or soot, and work as smoothly as they ever did. Clean whatever you can reach with a long-handled soft brush. Paint any areas that were painted but have become worn; if they are areas that are subject to heat, you should probably use stove paint. If you are not sure, write the manufacturer for instructions. If doors, spark screens, andirons, or grates have become warped, have them replaced. If there is any visible masonry (in the firebox interior, for instance), examine it to make sure it is sound; crumbled or soft masonry or fireclay liners should be replaced.

Fireplace Stoves

Cast iron stoves. Fireplace stoves should be maintained just like freestanding stoves. Cast-iron stoves may crack; doors may become loose-fitting. You can easily check for cracks by building a paper fire. Paper will light up the firebox with large flames. Examine all sides of the stove from the outside. If there is any sign of the fire—a crack need not be large—that part of the stove should be replaced. Remove any rust before inspecting for cracks; rust may conceal cracks.

In replacing plates on cast-iron stoves, be sure to allow for heat expansion of the parts. If you do not allow room for expansion, the stove may crack in the middle of a hot fire. If the components fit together with interlocking joints, clean all surfaces before replacing any parts. Air leakage through spaces left by poorly fitted parts can create undesirable drafts and too hot a fire. If the space is large enough, flames may be driven outside the stove by reversed air pressure, caused by a downdraft. Test the stove for tightness whenever you have replaced or repaired any parts.

Steel stoves. There are many grades of steel stoves, from the so-called tin stoves to those made of heavy plate steel, but any steel stove may burn out if abused. To guard against this, never build too hot a fire.

Once a year, inspect the stove inside and out for thin spots. Pay particular attention to areas that have become discolored, though this is not necessarily an indication that a thin spot has developed. To find a thin spot, press the outside with the heel of your hand, hard enough to try to flex the metal. A heavy-gauge stove will not flex at all unless there is a thin spot. Lighter gauges may flex a little; look for differences. If one area flexes more than another, you have probably found a thin spot. While it is possible to repair some steel stoves, it is not a good idea unless you have it inspected professionally, because one thin area indicates there may be others that are not as far gone but will be dangerous if used for another winter season.

Steel stoves may be spot welded; inspect these joins especially carefully since they are subject to more stress and could be opened by excessively hot fires. Continuous welding is more desirable and less liable to cause problems.

Inserts

Inserts must be removed at least once a year so that the chimney can be cleaned. Some homeowners store the insert out of the way and use the open fireplace during the summer months. Storing your insert in a dry place may prolong its life, because it cuts down on out-of-season rust formation, caused by rain coming down the chimney or moisture condensing in and behind the unit at a time when the drying effect of the fire is not available.

Once your unit is out of the fireplace, and before replacing it or storing it for the summer, inspect it thoroughly—especially the back—for rust. If you find any, remove it with a wire brush, finishing up with fine steel wool for a smoother surface. Use stove paint to touch up—it might not even be a bad idea to give the entire unit a light coating; this will take care of minute scratches and chips that otherwise might eventually rust. If you are not planning to use your unit for the summer months and if it has a grate, some manufacturers recommend storing the grate vertically, against the back of the firebox. An even better idea is to clean it thoroughly and wrap it in waterproof plastic.

Check door gaskets and sealing material for flues; replace if necessary (try to use the same material as before, or consult your dealer as to equivalent materials).

Firebrick

Firebrick lining will not endure indefinitely. If you use your stove regularly during the season, do not expect the firebrick to last more than five years; it may do so, but you should inspect it carefully each season to make sure it is still firm, compact, and in generally good condition. Firebrick liners in stoves are usually just set in, without any mortar, and can easily be removed and replaced by prying up the first brick—like getting olives out of a bottle. Make a diagram of how the bricks were placed and you will save yourself a great deal of time later trying to fit in the new ones.

Rust

Rust is the natural enemy of metal and your stove must be cleaned of it each season. Rust develops from moisture; there is nothing you can do to protect your stove from moisture, because even the fuel you are burning contains it. Seasoned hardwood contains 20 percent moisture; coal contains various amounts depending on many factors. If you do not maintain a fire all winter, any fuel left in the stove between fires will both absorb and give off moisture. Rain will come down the chimney occasionally; humid air in an unheated room will affect the exterior. Any stove not in use is liable to rust. For this reason, no matter how carefully you have serviced the stove at the end of the season, give it another quick inspection before lighting your first fire in the fall; rust may have developed over the summer.

Fortunately, rust is easily treated if caught before it has gone too far. Rub all rusty areas with fine steel wool. If the rust is very bad, you may have to use a wire brush to start with, but be sure not to scratch sound metal. After you have removed all the rust, wipe the stove down thoroughly with a soft cloth. At this point, manufacturers differ as to what they recommend. One suggests lightly oiling the surface of the stove for summer storage. Others say to spray the stove with a stove paint, such as Thurmalox 270 heat-resistant spray paint.

Blowers

The blower motor should, ideally, be vacuumed at least twice a year to keep it free of dust. If the motor is located in the front or side of the unit, this is easy to do; if it is in the back, you may have to wait until the unit is taken out for servicing and for cleaning the chimney. If, however, you notice any decline in blower efficiency, suspect that it may be clogging up. Do not continue to use the blower if it seems to be malfunctioning; you may damage it beyond repair.

Blowers require periodic lubrication, as do all motors. Here again, this should be done every six months. Use electric motor oil or, as recommended by some manufacturers, 10W or 20W nondetergent oil. Follow the manufacturer's directions for lubricating blower motors; your unit may have special requirements.

Clean the blower housing, as well as any grilles or vents, at the same time that you service the motor. Screens are particularly liable to build up dust; they are easily cleaned.

Exhaust Dampers

If it is possible to close off the chimney by closing the exhaust damper, do so when you are planning not to use your unit for a long period of time. Do not, of course, ever do this unless the fire is completely out. To be absolutely sure, wait until you have removed all the ashes.

Stovepipe

Stovepipe will need to be replaced every so often. Give it the test for thin spots (described above in the section on fireplace stoves), and inspect it for rust. Don't take chances with stovepipe; it's better to replace it before it is absolutely necessary than to risk a fire because of a burn-out.

Stove Cement

Many stoves are sealed with stove cement where plates or parts meet. This can shrink or crack and loosen or fall out, leaving openings through which flames can come into the room. Test with a screwdriver or similar tool to make sure that all cement is firmly in place. If it is not, pry it out and replace (this is easy to do).

Maintaining Viewing Glass

Types of Viewing Glass

In reading the specifications for the units described in Part Four, you will soon notice that the viewing windows are made of various kinds of glass. Many of the brand names—such as Vycor—that you will encounter are made by Corning Glass Works. Where only "tempered glass" is specified, it may or may not be a name brand. If you want to know, ask the dealer.

Corning is very concerned with the development of glass for domestic burners, heaters, and fireplace inserts and has several studies in the works. Possibly there are other manufacturers likewise engaged and you should pay attention to what kind of glass is used in your unit and what claims are made for it. Since glass breakage can occur even with the best glass made, do anything you can to minimize this problem.

You can, of course, avoid it altogether by using metal doors, but then you will lose the view of the fire at least most of the time. Another option is to buy a stove, such as Scotland's Esse, that uses mica instead of glass. Mica is a natural mineral that is semitransparent and that was much used instead of glass in the nineteenth century. It is heat resistant and will not break.

The most important characteristic of viewing glass is its resistance to heat. Since the heat within the firebox can be considerable, greater resistance to heat adds an element of safety—especially for the homeowner who is new to wood-burning and may build too hot a fire during the learning process. For coal stoves, with their much higher firebox heat, only the most heat-resistant glass should be used. Even then, extreme care should be taken in managing the fire so that only normal heat is generated.

It is important, also, to use dry fuel. If too much fresh fuel is added to a going fire and if the moisture content is high, the firebox will fill with steam. In the case of a coal fire, the steam will be extremely acid; so much so that when it condenses, a drop falling onto your bare hand might cause an acid burn.

A look at the range of Corning glass will acquaint you with what you may find in the stoves on the market. These include: Vycor, Pyroceram, Pyrex borosilicate (both tempered and plain), and soda lime (both tempered and plain). The two most important characteristics of each type are the amount of heat resistance and the coefficient of thermal expansion.

Vycor is the most suitable material for high heat levels, such as that produced by a coal fire. It is 96 percent silica and, in Corning's words, "will handle any anticipated temperature and thermal shock that may be produced in a wood or coal burning heater . . . much higher than any that may be generated in a woodburning stove or fireplace. Splashes of water or snow on the glass surface are not a concern."

The next-highest grade is Pyroceram, which Corning describes as "a transparent glass ceramic with thermal properties somewhat below those of Vycor glass but well above Pyrex glass . . . will handle the thermal abuse of most woodstove and fireplace applications."

The Pyroceram glass is smooth on one side but slightly patterned on the other; its amber tint does not detract from the view of the fire. In Corning's view, the patterning "sparkles" in log flames and hides the view of ashes when the fire is out. If you want to decide whether you like the effect of this glass (which you might not have noticed if I hadn't mentioned it), bring a candle in a candlestick to your stove dealer's. Light the candle and put it in the firebox with the doors closed.

Pyrex brand glass is, of course, the kind that pots and pans are made of. It is a borosilicate glass that "will handle most any thermal shock that may normally be encountered at operating temperatures less than 550 degrees F."

When buying a stove or insert with a glass window, you trust that the manufacturer has used a type of glass that is appropriate for the amount of heat produced in his unit. Design is an important consideration because such factors as air vents located in the immediate vicinity of the glass (where they might shock the glass) could cause problems that would not ordinarily arise.

You are not, however, completely dependent on the manufacturer's experience and integrity if you confine your purchases to stoves with industry approvals. One of the tests commonly performed before a label or listing is issued is an impact test, in which a metal ball is swung against the glass to test how easily and in what way it shatters. Since the test is a carry-over from storm-door-glass testing, it is not completely applicable to viewing glass, but at the moment, it is the best we have. An example of the inappropriateness

PHYSICAL PROPERTIES

Table 1

1/4" Thick Materials	°F Normal Service	°F Extreme Service	°F Max. Thermal Shock	°F Max Thermal Gradient	In/In/°F Coefficient of Thermal Expansion	PSI Design Tensile
VYCOR® 96% Silica Code 7913	1652	2192	1800	396	4.2×10^{-7}	1000
PYROCERAM™ Trans-parent Glass-Ceramic Code 9618	1202	1382	1400	450	3.3×10^{-7}	1500
Tempered PYREX® Borosilicate Code 7740	500	554	580	194	18×10^{-7}	2000
PYREX® Borosilicate Code 7740	446	914	270	97	18×10^{-7}	1000
Soda-Lime Tempered Code 0080	428	482	366	88	52×10^{-7}	3000
Soda-Lime Code 0080	230	860	122	29	52×10^{-7}	1000

Normal Service —
   No breakage from excessive thermal shock is assumed. Nonabused glass should last indefinitely.

Extreme Limits —
   The glass will be very vulnerable to thermal shock and physical degradation. Recommendations in this range are based on mechanical stability considerations only. Tests should be made before adopting final designs. These data approximate only.

Thermal Shock —
   The physical shock glass undergoes when evenly heated to the above listed temperature, then plunged into water at 50°F without breakage. This data approximate only and varies with thickness.

Temperature Gradient —
   The difference in temperature between the two surfaces that will cause 1000 psi tensile stress on the cooler surface.

Coefficient of Thermal Expansion —
   The relative increase in size of a material when heated.

Tensile Strength —
   The resistance of a material to breakage under the stress of pulling or stretching.

Design Tensile Strength —
   The anticipated tensile load that a material can withstand over an indefinite period of time.

Table from "Selection and Installation Handbook for Glass in Fireplaces and Woodburning Stoves," BY CORNING GLASS WORKS.

of this type of test is that the glass is considered more desirable if it shatters into tiny pieces rather than cracking into larger pieces that stay in place. The tiny pieces may be desirable with storm doors, but with viewing glass it is probably preferable and safer if the glass cracks in place (where it will contain the fire, at least for a while).

If all this causes you some concern, look for the unit that adds a mesh screen for additional protection. The screen is usually mounted between the glass and the fire and acts both to protect the glass from falling logs and as a spark guard if the glass breaks. Mesh screens are more noticeable when there is no fire in the firebox, so do not be put off by one and think it will spoil your view of the fire. Here, again, the candle test will provide a more accurate idea of the visibility of the flame through the mesh/glass combination. I do not think most people will find it objectionable.

Care of Viewing Glass

Never forget that viewing glass is breakable; assume that a certain amount of breakage is inevitable and think about this before you purchase your stove or insert. No matter what the stove dealer may tell you, if you note that most manufacturers—even those with long-term warranties—do not warranty the glass against breakage, you will realize how common a problem breakage is. A few do offer a one-year warranty on glass and say they have not had any customers submit a claim for breakage, but this is the exception.

There are two common causes of glass breakage. One, which is entirely within your control, is jarring or banging against the glass with a log or a poker. A little care on the part of the person managing the fire will eliminate this kind of occurrence. Children will, of course, be taught to keep away from the stove or insert; when they are old enough to help in managing it, they should be taught how.

Another common cause is a burning log falling against the glass from inside the firebox. The fire should always be built in such a way that the logs will fall down toward the floor of the firebox; they should not be perched so precariously or at such an angle that they will fall forward. Not only is the glass liable to break if touched by a burning log; you are liable to have a problem if you attempt to open a front-loading door when burning logs are leaning against it. Many manufacturers will recommend that you build your fire as much toward the back of the firebox as possible to eliminate this problem. Some stoves are designed so that the firebox slants toward the middle and logs automatically slide down to the center as they burn.

Glass will also tend to break if you build too hot a fire. Inexperienced stove owners, eager to get maximum heat production, often build too high a fire and run it too hot. If your stove has a firebrick lining, the logs should not be stacked above the bricks. A firebox should never be filled to the top with wood; such overloading may damage the firebox, cause the stovepipe to get too hot, and send too many sparks up the chimney (to land on the roof, perhaps, and cause a roof fire). Be patient. A properly built fire will give you more heat than an overstacked blaze, and is certainly much safer.

Follow directions (see next section) for cleaning so that you do not damage the glass in the process.

When you are considering the purchase of a stove or an insert, ask how you can remove the glass for cleaning or in the event of breakage. If the stove dealer doesn't know, study the literature; it may tell you. If you still can't find out, read the installation instructions—the information is usually there. It is much easier to clean the glass when you can lay it on a flat surface than if you have to reach into the firebox, or even if you can open the doors wide but still have to do it in the vertical position. Often the entire door can be simply lifted off the hinges. Sometimes the glass slides out easily. If you are having trouble deciding between two stoves, this factor should be taken into consideration.

Try not to touch the glass with anything when it is hot. Be especially careful not to touch it with anything cold or wet. A log brought in from outside may have ice or snow on it; it should not be allowed to touch the glass or the outside of the stove.

Get in the habit of inspecting the glass regularly—every morning or evening, for example. In this way, you will be likely to spot a crack just as it is beginning and can take prompt steps to have it replaced before it becomes dangerous. If you cannot put the fire out immediately (difficult with a coal fire), and if it does not have protective wire mesh behind it, place a fire screen in front of it and let the fire die down. *Do not use a unit if the glass is cracked.*

Try not to splash water on hot glass. The shock may break it. Cold drafts can have the same effect, so be careful of open windows on a cold day.

Open and close the doors gently. Slamming the door when the glass is hot may cause stresses it cannot resist.

All these cautions may lead you to think that glass is basically an unsafe material for a wood- or coal-burning unit. It isn't at all; properly installed in a suitably designed stove, glass can be almost as durable as it is beautiful. An understanding of its properties—such as increased brittleness when hot—will help you to enjoy the fire safely and comfortably through the viewing windows, and to deal promptly with any problems that may arise.

Cleaning Viewing Glass

Anyone who has ever had a glass viewing window on an oven door knows how soon it can be covered with a build-up that makes it impossible to see what is happening inside the oven, and that looks unsightly from the outside. The same sort of problem arises with the viewing windows of fireplace stoves—although for a somewhat different reason—and most of them require frequent cleaning if visibility is to be retained.

Cleaning viewing glass is a chore that should be done frequently. It is important, aside from the unattractive appearance of dirty glass, because the build-up becomes increasingly difficult to remove the longer it is allowed to form; it can even reach the point where it is almost as impervious as porcelain enamel, and nothing short of a blowtorch will remove it. In this event, the see-through feature is lost completely.

How to clean the glass has, however, proved to be a problem. A mixture of ammonia and detergent may serve to remove early deposits, but most of the time will not prove sufficiently strong. I surveyed a number of manufacturers of fireplace stoves and inserts, as well as Corning Glass Works, and here are some of their suggestions regarding cleaning agents.

1. A mild abrasive powder, such as Bon Ami. Under no circumstances use a harsh powder.

2. A commercial product made for this purpose, such as Butcher's. I checked Butcher's with some insert owners who had used it, and they found it satisfactory.

3. Oven cleaner. This works quite well but requires more care than Butcher's because it is caustic. It removes even thick, baked-on deposits fairly easily, and is a product you probably already have in your cupboard so you don't have to buy it specially. I would suggest you use the brush-on rather than the spray type, since the spray may get onto materials other than the glass, and oven cleaners are not recommended for some metals. With the brush-on, you have more control. Follow meticulously the manufacturer's directions for use.

When I spoke to consultants at Corning about the use of oven cleaners on their various types of viewing glass, they said they were satisfactory but, being caustic, should be used with extreme care. Oven cleaner, they said, if left on during the next firing, can permanently stain the glass as well as damage the finish on metal. They told me of a customer who had opened the door of his fireplace insert, sprayed it with oven cleaner and then closed it again while he went about other chores. When he came back, the glass was totally white; the cleaner had leached the glass and formed a permanent finish that could not be removed. The only recourse was to replace the glass. Corning urgently warns stove owners not to clean the glass while it is hot, not to leave the cleaner on for any length of time, and to rinse thoroughly with clear water.

Don't use steel wool. I have had desperate homeowners tell me that they couldn't find anything else that worked (they hadn't tried some of the above suggestions), so they resorted to steel wool. Steel wool will work, but it is tedious and will eventually cause problems. Steel wool used on glass tends to cause tiny scratches—they can be so fine that you can't even see them. These scratches gradually cover more and more of the glass and affect visibility. In addition, they weaken the glass and make it more liable to crack. Even if you have used steel wool successfully to remove paint and other deposits from window glass, do not use it on glass that is exposed to heat.

Go easy on razor blades. Most homeowners have used a razor blade at one time or another to clean their house windows, especially to clean up paint and putty. If you have a particularly stubborn area of deposit on your viewing window, you may be tempted to resort to a razor blade. As long as the blade removes the deposit *without touching the glass,* it is safe. The danger, however, is that you will inadvertently get down to the glass, in which case you will scratch it with the blade just as you will with steel wool—and the scratches will be more noticeable. A better solution is to put on another application of oven cleaner; it may take a little longer, but it is much safer.

Never clean glass when it is hot. No matter what method you use, the glass should be allowed to cool down considerably before you attempt to clean it. You will find that it is easier to clean if it is warm—cold glass cleans only with great difficulty—but it should not be too hot to handle comfortably with bare hands.

Rinse glass thoroughly. After you have cleaned the glass, rinse it thoroughly with clear warm water. No residue of the cleaner should remain on the glass. If using oven cleaner that requires rinsing with a vinegar/water mixture, follow with a plain water rinse.

Dry and polish glass. Do not leave the glass wet. It will streak and may crack if the water cools rapidly and the fire heats up quickly.

Before building your first fire, perhaps spray the inside window with a silicone product, such as Pam. This is one manufacturer's suggestion for easier cleaning; I haven't tried it, but he says it works.

Reducing Build-up

No matter what you do, the glass will eventually need cleaning, but there are a few things you can do to minimize the build-up and darkening of the window.

Burn dry wood. You should anyhow, because wet wood will give less heat and will cause more creosote formation in your chimney; it will also mess up your glass more quickly. You won't have to clean so often if you burn dry wood.

Don't bank or damper down your fire unnecessarily. Every time you do, you increase creosote build-up in your chimney and deposit more material on your glass. Running a good fire with the drafts open for an hour or so may take care of the chimney, but chances are it won't do much to restore visibility to the glass.

Viewing Glass Breakage

Stove dealers, like doctors, don't make house calls. If the viewing glass breaks —and you should assume it will—will you be able to deal with it yourself? This is a question you should learn the answer to *before you complete your purchase.*

If you are installing your own unit, you are probably capable of taking it

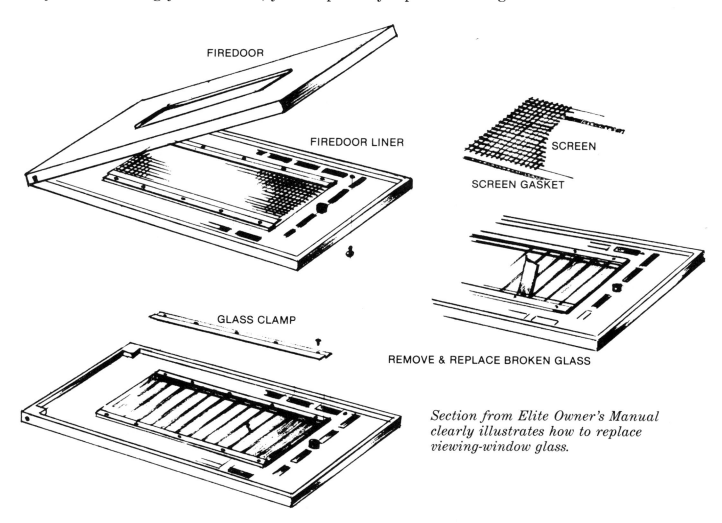

Section from Elite Owner's Manual clearly illustrates how to replace viewing-window glass.

apart when necessary. If you're having it installed, its components may be something of a mystery to you. Ideally, however, removing and replacing broken glass should not be an arduous task. The glass should be fitted into the unit in such a way that it can be removed merely by sliding it out, by taking out a few screws, or in some similarly easy manner. Changing the glass should not be so difficult that you put it off; broken viewing glass is dangerous because the glass contains the fire. If your viewing glass shatters and falls out, your fire is no longer safely contained and presents a hazard. For this reason, some manufacturers put a safety screen between the glass and the outside of the viewing window. This obscures slightly your view of the fire, but it ensures that the fire will never be a hazard.

Another safety device found in some units is a metal panel that can be put into place in front of the glass when the fire is banked for the night.

One aspect of possible viewing glass breakage that homeowners new to this kind of unit often fail to take into account is the fact that a broken viewing window may mean that the unit cannot be used until the glass has been replaced. If the dealer is temporarily out of stock of the glass for your unit, you may find yourself unable to use the stove for several weeks—just at a time when you need it most. Some manufacturers offer a metal replacement panel as an option. If your unit comes with this option, I would strongly recommend that you order the metal replacement panel or panels right away. It is little enough to pay for insurance that your stove will always be usable even if the glass breaks. This is just as true even if your dealer assures you he always carries replacement glass, since breakage may occur when his store is closed; you would have to put out the fire and wait until business hours to obtain new glass.

If the glass should crack or break and you do not have a metal panel or protective screen, you should immediately allow the fire to go out (close downdraft controls to speed the process unless it is a cool fire), and stay in the room until the fire is quite low.

Caution: If you are burning coal instead of wood, and the glass breaks, do not bank or smother the fire. Burn it down as quickly as possible, adding sufficient secondary air so that gases will not seep into the room. If you want to speed the process and save the coal, shovel it into a metal coal bucket, which should have a cover, as soon as the flames have died down, and put the bucket *outdoors.* Do not leave it on an enclosed porch or other area close to the house.

In replacing the glass, it is important to be sure that it is not under stress when it is in position.

1. Check the surface that touches the glass (or covers it) to make sure it is flat and smooth; if the frame has become distorted during use, it may keep breaking the glass by stressing it.
2. Allow ⅛ inch clearance around the edge of the glass; the thermal expansion of the metal frame requires more room than when the frame is cold.
3. Be sure you can move the glass in the frame (see illustration); if you cannot, either the glass is too large or something is wrong with the way you have replaced it.

If you have the glass replaced and it breaks again shortly after, try to determine the cause. It may be the way you are managing the fire; it may be an unsuitable type of glass; it may be failure to observe the above three points. If the dealer is inexperienced, he may make a mistake without meaning to; it is up to you to work with him to solve the problem.

15

How to Burn Solid Fuel Safely

Containing the Fire

Several years ago, in *Fortune* magazine, the twenty things commonly to be found around the house were listed in order of danger. Except for space heaters, most of the items were things like bathtubs, basketballs, furniture, and showers. Wood stoves ranked about twentieth. The ranking might be higher if the study were to be done today, because today there are more wood stoves in use; but mostly, danger is not inherent in the items but results from the way they are used. A bathtub is not in itself dangerous; accidents occur when consumers fail to allow for the fact that a soapy wet bathtub will be slippery. This is a predictable condition and steps can easily be taken to deal with it. So it is with burning solid fuel. Most fires that are caused by wood or coal stoves are actually the result of the homeowner's failure to take simple, sensible precautions.

The primary factors that determine safe use of any domestic fuel are containment and control of the fire. To a large extent, containment is assured by the purchase of heating equipment that is built to certain recognized standards. The average consumer can make sure the unit conforms to these standards by buying one with a testing laboratory label, such as UL, Arnold Greene Laboratories, or the many others in the field. As we said earlier, a standardized, nationally accepted label would greatly simplify the consumer's choice. At present, however, there are no industry standards at all for inserts, but this situation may be remedied in the near future. The Fireplace Institute in its testing laboratories at Auburn University does rate the energy performance of inserts, built-ins, and similar wood-burning units. Primarily, the institute establishes an Efficiency Rating, and its label gives the heat output in BTU's per hour, based on an input fuel rate in pounds of dry wood per hour, and room airflow of number of cubic feet per minute. These "output to input" labels are similar to air conditioner labels and are helpful in estimating how much wood a unit will use and how much heat (BTU production) you can expect from the unit. The Fireplace Institute label replaces the manufacturers' estimates of BTU production and is probably more reliable, simply because it is done by an independent laboratory testing all units under similar conditions.

You should realize that these ratings are good for comparison purposes, but will not necessarily hold true when the unit is installed in your home. How well any stove or heating device will work in a specific situation depends on many variables, such as drafts, room layout, insulation, placement of fireplace, height of ceiling, and so on. The Fireplace Institute label is meant to supplement, not to replace, labels that rate the efficiency, safety, and utility of heat-producing units.

The consumer can further ensure the safe containment of a fire by safe installation. This includes having the chimney cleaned and inspected before the unit is put in place, and having the chimney, pipe, and unit cleaned at least once a year thereafter. It includes making installations in strict conformance with state and local building codes as well as using appropriate pipe—stovepipe, prefab chimney pipe, etc.—in such a manner and in proper gauge, with industry approval labels to ensure that you are getting what you are paying for.

Safe containment includes checking the unit annually for servicing, replacing cracked viewing glass, cracked cast-iron plates, and sprung welded steel joints. It includes attention to details, such as bolting stovepipe together and making sure baffle plates, if any, and other in-stove areas are cleaned when the chimney is cleaned. Safe containment includes keeping children away from the fire and making sure door latches are working properly so that doors will not open accidentally.

Containment of the fire by all these mechanical methods is not difficult. It means, basically, making sure that the firebox—whether within the fireplace or in a fireplace stove on the hearth—will not let the fire wander outside of its chamber and will not vent the burning volatiles anywhere except up the chimney. In the case of coal burning, this latter point is especially important since the volatiles may include poisonous gases, such as carbon monoxide. With a wood fire, all you need worry about is the flames and burning wood. With a coal fire, it is the gases that are more dangerous; the flames tend to be short and the coal is less liable to fall out of the stove.

Controlling the Fire

The fire should never burn too hot. Some homeowners are their own worst enemy in this respect because they do not understand how to manage a fire and think the more fuel and the hotter the fire the better. They choke the fire chamber with wood or coal so that it cannot burn efficiently, and they open the draft controls so much that most of the heat is drawn up the chimney. This is hard on the firebox, hard on the stovepipe, hard on the chimney; it is also dangerous. Follow the manufacturer's instructions as well as those in this book and learn to be sensible about building and running the fire.

Managing a Chimney Fire

A chimney fire is both dangerous and frightening, a bad combination because when you are frightened it is hard to remember to do the things in the proper order.

A chimney fire is not inevitable. If you keep your chimney clean and do not burn your fire too hot, chances are you will never have this experience. Chimney fires are caused by soot and creosote in the flue catching on fire. There are some new theories about creosote formation, but they have not been fully

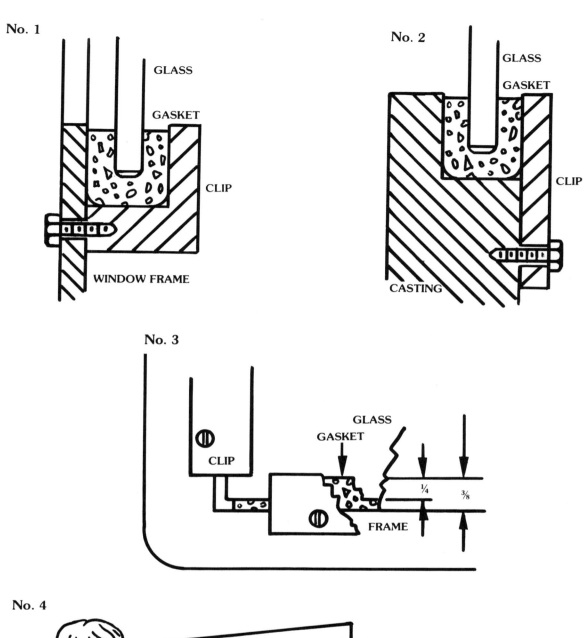

No. 1

GLASS

GASKET

CLIP

WINDOW FRAME

No. 2

GLASS

GASKET

CLIP

CASTING

No. 3

CLIP

GLASS

GASKET

FRAME

¼

⅜

No. 4

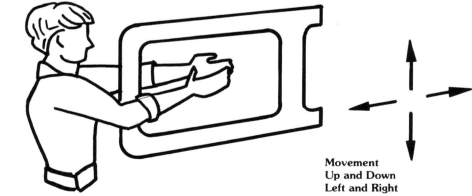

Movement
Up and Down
Left and Right

Page from "Selection and Installation Handbook for Glass in Fireplaces and Woodburning Stoves," BY CORNING GLASS WORKS, *illustrating gasketing of viewing glass and movement in proper installation.*

checked out, so for the present I would suggest you follow the old guidelines for minimizing creosote build-up.

1. Burn dry, seasoned hardwood.
2. Do not run a slow fire any longer than you have to.
3. Follow any period of a slow fire (as overnight) with at least twenty minutes with the fire burning at peak levels. This will tend to burn off the soot and creosote that have formed during the slow burning period.
4. Do not burn trash unless the manufacturer specifically says it is all right—and maybe not even then.
5. Burn as little softwood, especially resinous wood, as possible.
6. Check your stovepipe to see if you are getting excessive creosote build-up. You should not need to clean the chimney more than once a year; if you are building up creosote so fast that you need clean-outs much oftener than that, try to figure out what you are doing wrong. Occasionally, a chimney may stay too cool (due to location on an outside wall of the house, for instance), and this is a factor you cannot change and will just have to adjust your cleaning schedule to.

It is best if the entire household has been briefed on what to do in the event of a chimney fire. If there are two people in the house, one should immediately *call the fire department* and the other should *close the draft controls* so that oxygen will be cut off from the fire. You need the fire department as soon as possible. A chimney fire burns so hot (as hot as 2000 degrees F.) that it can crack even a sound chimney flue, and flames may then reach combustible material. In addition, it will create sparks, which can set the roof and surrounding shrubbery or trees on fire.

Here are the warning signs that you have a fire in the chimney:

1. Sucking sounds
2. Shaking stovepipe and flue pipe
3. A loud roar

Of the three, the roaring sound is the most frightening, and no one who has heard it ever forgets it. At the first hint of any of these signs, *call the fire department.* The phone number should be on or next to every phone in the house.

Safety Devices

Keep a class A *fire extinguisher* handy to the stove. Read the instructions carefully and go over them once a month with everyone in the house; even a twelve-year-old can learn to use a fire extinguisher. Do not just put it up and forget it. Check every so often, according to manufacturer's instructions, to make sure it is still in working condition.

Install smoke detectors. You may have smoke before the fire bursts into flames. A smoke detector should be located in the room with the stove and in a nearby or upstairs area. It will smell smoke before you do, and will alert everyone in the house much more quickly than you could. Be sure everyone understands clearly what to do if the alarm goes off. It might be a good idea to have an occasional fire drill to make sure that everyone knows how to get out of the house quickly in case of a fire. If one of the exits is a window, be sure it opens easily and is not blocked by hard-to-move objects.

If you burn coal, install a volatiles detector. It will quickly detect odorless, colorless, smokeless gases which may be fatal if allowed to accumulate. If a volatiles detector goes off, immediately open as many doors and windows as possible. Put a handkerchief over your nose and quickly open the draft controls, especially the secondary draft control, if there is one, on the stove. Then go outside. After ten minutes or so, turn off the alarm. If the air is safe to breathe, the alarm will not go on again. If it does go on again, stay outside a while longer, and continue to air the house.

Watch for these symptoms of carbon monoxide poisoning:
1. Headache
2. Weakness
3. Nausea
4. Fainting
5. Paralysis of nervous system
6. Slow pulse
7. Slow respiration

Remember: the immediate treatment is fresh air. If symtoms persist, call the ambulance.

Ash Disposal

Fires are easily started by careless ash disposal. Most ashes contain some hot coals; wood ashes cool faster than coal ashes, but even wood ashes can retain enough heat to start a fire for several hours after they have been taken out of the firebox. Coal ashes may have living coals for much longer than that.

Ashes should always be put in a covered metal container. Coal ash buckets should be put outdoors immediately. Both wood and coal ash containers should never be put on a wood floor or on any combustible surface.

Do not dispose of the ashes in an ash bucket until you are sure they are completely dead. If they are even warm to the bare hand, do not tip them out of the bucket. You may think it is safe to dispose of ashes if you bury them, but this can be the most dangerous method of all. Forest fires are often difficult to put out because tree roots catch on fire and the fire smolders underground, only to surface unexpectedly some distance from the original site of the fire. If you bury hot ashes and they happen to be near tree roots, this can happen to you. Never bury ashes unless they are *cold*. This is especially important with coal ashes because they accumulate so much faster than wood ashes, especially if you are burning a low-rank coal. You may find you need two ash buckets for convenience sake. Wood ashes are an excellent addition to a compost heap or may be spread directly on your lawn or garden.

Fuel Selection

Burn only the fuel the manufacturer recommends for the unit. If the manual says wood and lignite, do not burn anthracite. It will make a hotter fire than the unit can take.

Do not burn trash unless the manufacturer specifically says you can.

Do not burn driftwood if the manufacturer says not to.

Do not use commercial fire starters, such as those made for starting barbecue fires. Do not use starters such as gasoline, or any other volatile liquid. Use only paper and kindling.

Do not use fuel with wax binders; many manufactured fuel logs are dangerous to burn in enclosed spaces. Be sure you know which ones are safe.

Packaged Coal and Wood Products

As we have already noted, coal may be bought in bags from stove dealers and some hardware stores. Try to get anthracite if your unit can burn it. If all that is available is bituminous, be sure you are not paying anthracite prices for it. If both 50- and 100-pound bags are available, the larger amount should be proportionately cheaper; you will still be paying a considerable premium over the price per ton.

In addition to this type of coal, you may be offered manufactured coal/wood combinations. CoalLog, a brand-name product, is sometimes available. It is shaped like a log and formed of a shell of compressed wood chips filled with a center of bituminous coal. There are many similar "logs" or "bricks" on the market that combine coal and wood in various proportions.

Coal briquets, except for a lignite briquet imported from West Germany, are usually made of a high-ranked bituminous coal, and in the process of manufacture lose much of their ash and sulfur content, which makes them more desirable.

You will also find numerous compressed-wood products that contain no coal. Be careful of the binders, which may be unsafe except for open fires.

All these man-made fuel materials are pulverized and then compressed into uniform shapes—logs, bricks, pellets—for easy handling. They are much cleaner than coal, handier and more compact than natural wood logs, and frequently much easier to ignite. They are also generally more expensive than the raw product (wood or coal), but since they use sawdust, wood chips, and other waste materials, it is conceivable that they will become much less expensive if there is an increased demand for them.

If you try to use the pellets in your standard coal grate, you may run into a problem because they are fairly small and may soon fall between the grate supports into the ashpan or ashbed. Perhaps the manufacturers could be alerted to this problem and could increase the size of the pellets. Until that is done, however, you will have to adapt your grate in some way to accommodate the small size of the burning pellet.

A Word of Caution

The products described above should not be used indiscriminately. Follow the manufacturer's instructions as to what his unit will burn. If a unit will burn only wood, do not use a coal/wood combination.

Even if your unit is designed for both wood and coal, some manufactured fuel may be unsuitable for anything but an open fireplace. Cosmetic logs that are designed to produce colorful flames are usually unsafe to use in an enclosed firebox or behind glass doors. Many of the packaged coal and wood products should be used only in certain types of fireboxes. If in doubt, do not use them.

Do not depend entirely on the advice of salespeople. The local branch of a large chain recently displayed one of their stoves with wax logs piled inside in the typical fireplace pyramid. The implication was that those logs could be used in the stove. I mentioned to the manager that this was a dangerous

INDUSTRY APPROVALS, LISTINGS, AND LABELS

At the moment, industry approvals and labeling are in a fairly chaotic state because there is no single nationally accepted label. What has happened, instead, is that individual states—such as Massachusetts, Maine, and Connecticut—have set up their own standards and in some cases require that the unit be tested by a specified laboratory in that state. Massachusetts, for example, requires the label of Arnold Greene Laboratories, testing to UL standards, on stoves sold within the state. Industries, state and federal governments, all realize that this is an unsatisfactory and costly system and they are working together to remedy it. Meanwhile, excellent stoves, built to the most exacting standards, may not be acceptable within your state. A European stove may have the DIN label, from West Germany, which means it has been built for less clearance to combustibles than the usual 36 inches and is certified as safe under those conditions by strict standards, but it still will not be accepted in Massachusetts unless it has the Arnold Greene listing. Similarly, a French stove with the UFACD label from the French industrial association will not be acceptable in Massachusetts without local testing, even though the French listing means the stove has tested out to be over 70 percent efficient, and has a proven burn time of at least twelve hours on not more than one quarter the normal fuel load.

Until a national label exists, be sure the stove you want to buy will be issued an installation permit in your state. Here are some of the many labels and listings you will encounter.

ACIL	American Council of Independent Laboratories
ASTM	American Society for Testing and Material
BOCA	Building Officials and Code Administrators International
CABO	Conference of American Building Officials
CSA	Canadian Standards Association
DIN	West Germany industry approval
FI	Fireplace Institute (testing lab at Auburn University, Auburn, Alabama)
ICBO	International Conference of Building Code Officials
NBS	National Bureau of Standards
SBCCI	Southern Building Code Congress International
UFACD	French Association of Manufacturers of Home Heating Appliances
UL	Underwriters Laboratories
WEI	Wood Energy Institute

display inasmuch as the logs were unsafe for that use, whereas the consumer might be led to believe they were suitable. The manager assured me that he never told anyone to use those logs in the stoves he was selling, and that the display was intended only to be decorative. I spoke to one of the salesmen and *he* thought the logs were fine and took the display literally. Read the manufacturer's instructions; they are your best guide and most manufacturers will prominently display any cautions regarding inappropriate fuels.

Keep Yourself Safe

Safety is largely up to you. In New England there is a saying: "It's impossible to make anything foolproof; fools are too ingenious." Don't outsmart yourself by taking shortcuts. Don't be too busy to read all the instructions and manuals the manufacturer gives you. Don't hesitate to ask questions about anything that is not clear to you. Once you learn how to manage a fire, don't get careless. Fire is a good servant but a poor master in a firebox as well as in a forest. You have nothing to fear from a wood- or coal-burning unit as long as you take the obvious precautions and use your common sense.

Part Four

The Wood- and Coal-Burner's Catalog

How to Use this Catalog

All devices—fireplace stoves, inserts, built-ins, and grates—are listed alphabetically, along with accessories, such as fans, baking ovens, etc. At the end of the catalog, there is a listing of manufacturers with their addresses, so that you may write for brochures or manuals.

Each item is described in detail and specifications are given. Although no value judgments are made (because each heating situation is different and all devices are useful under appropriate circumstances), it is possible to determine, to some extent, which devices are more sturdily built, of high-quality materials, with above-average quality control. The specific materials listed are a useful indication of quality, and the manufacturer's warranty reflects to some extent his confidence in his own product as well as his expectations for it.

Bear in mind that most of the information has been provided by the manufacturer and is, therefore, to be viewed with the same slight skepticism with which the intelligent consumer approaches any item in the marketplace. On the other hand, facts are facts, and such items as construction materials are not subject to exaggeration or interpretation. As soon as all devices have industry approval labels, some of this element of risk will be removed from the purchase of heating equipment. A source of much controversy, when those in the trade talk among themselves, is the claims made for potential heat production. Here again, labeling will soon give those figures greater credibility, but they can never be used as an absolute guide. Many variables affect heat production and each installation is different. How well your house is insulated, how the floor plan lends itself to channeling hot air through the rooms, how draft-free your windows, exhaust fan outlets, and such are—all these factors will affect what any heating device can do to make you comfortable.

In addition, there is the question of how best to present heat production. You will notice the lack of uniformity: manufacturers give BTU production, quote number of cubic feet or square feet their unit will heat. Each manufacturer has reasons for the way he chooses to present this information. Many producers believe that BTU ratings should not be given because they can mislead the consumer as to the efficiency of a unit. David Linnet, of the Alaska Company, wrote me regarding this point: "We believe a BTU rating on a woodburning unit can be misleading because you can create such a high BTU output, but it will only last a short time. The secret behind woodburning is a low constant fire, easily maintained, and overall good efficiency." Over and over again, manufacturers have said that a roaring fire with high flames is not desirable, that it puts a strain on the unit and can cause damage, and that a lower fire—even a coal stage—is better and a more even heat producer. There is very little agreement in the field on this point; one point is clear, however. The natural tendency to pile on logs on a cold day should be checked; overloading the firebox or opening the draft to get the fire to burn hotter is liable to send more heat up the chimney than into the house.

You can use this catalog to determine what kind of heating device best suits your situation. The next step is to select those units in that category which look most attractive to you and are within your price range. Please note, however, that all prices are given for comparison purposes only; they are sure to be higher when you go shopping. On the other hand, if you wait until the middle to the end of the season, most retailers put all their stock on sale and you could conceivably buy some of these units below the price listed in this book.

I would suggest that before you go to look at the unit in a store, you make a chart for yourself, listing the name of the unit and its specifications. You can probably get all the units in which you are interested on one piece of paper and then can quickly compare to see which is larger, is more expensive, has more standard features, requires you to buy more options, takes a larger amount of fuel, has a longer burn time, etc. Any gaps—such as industry approvals that were still pending at press time—can be filled in at the retailer's. It's much better to write all of these facts down than to try to keep them in your head. Sometimes, also, you will be able to see at a glance that one unit has features which suit you better than any other; this could simplify your decision even if you are inexperienced with domestic heating devices.

If one dealer can't answer your questions, try another; you should shop around, in any case. If you still have questions, do not hesitate to call the manufacturer; he will be delighted to help you.

Aeroheator Householder

The Householder is the largest of the Aeroheator line; it may be larger than you need for the space you wish to heat, so you probably ought to look into the other two units. All Aeroheators are sold direct to the consumer and you can usually count on delivery within two weeks of sending out your order.

The Householder incorporates all the features of the original Aeroheator, designed by Alex Moncrieff-Yeates, but a few minor changes have been made. The Yeateses feel that the unit is now even easier to install, and they have found that a number of options are often requested, so they have added these to the line. In addition, of course, they now offer the basic unit in three sizes, with minor differences to be found among them.

In case you are not familiar with the Aeroheator, here are some of its features. It has a patented heat exchanger which operates on a vortex principle, so that the unit can heat an entire room within 15 minutes of lighting the fire and a much larger area a short time after. It operates without electricity, but because of the design, it feeds combustion air into the fire from underneath the logs, while convective air is recirculated through the unit, around the firebox, and into the room through a two-stage heat exchanger; there is no direct path from the fire to the chimney. Volatiles are heated to a much higher temperature than with an ordinary log fire; the completeness of the combustion is evident from the fine ash residue that remains. So little ash is formed that a unit in use 24 hours a day usually needs to have the ashes removed no more than once a week. In addition, the efficiency of the Householder is such that a three-time-a-day loading can keep the fire going around the clock. The designer claims the Aeroheator does not benefit from, or require, outside ducting since it uses so much less room air (because of the design) than the average fireplace.

The Yeateses are very fond of an open fire, so their unit is designed to be operated this way, and they claim it results in very little heat loss. They do, however, offer swing-back metal or glass doors, or a firescreen for those who want it. I, personally, would never feel safe with an open fire that was not—at least—behind a screen, and strongly recommend that you avail yourself of at least one of these options. They also offer a Quencher Door for

putting out the fire promptly—a fuel saver if you use the fireplace only part of the time.

The patented features of the Aeroheators have received considerable publicity and the photograph may look familiar to you because it was featured in a *NASA Activities* magazine article on woodburning heaters as a "woodburning heater . . . with little waste of energy . . ." The article also commented on the fact that the Aeroheator used Pyromark as a protective coating—a material that was used on Apollo mission spacecraft because it is capable of casting off, rather than absorbing, radiant energy, and protects against temperatures of up to 1800 degrees F. The photograph shows the Householder in use, and Susan Yeates wrote me: "Edwin, our cat, really fusses if we don't have the Aeroheator lit for him (that's Edwin in the photograph—the one not reading a book)."

SPECIFICATIONS

Dimensions: Custom fitted to existing masonry fireplaces

Materials: Steel plate, steel sheet, solid brass

Shipping weight: 150 lbs.

Heating capacity: 40,000 BTU's

Warranty: Limited 2-year warranty

Burn time: 20 hours

Options: Manual flue control, screen doors, glass doors, quencher doors, closure doors, deflector, decorative medallion, coal adapter

Approximate price: $695

© 1980 ALASKA CO. INC.

Alaska Kodiak Fireplace Insert

Except for the fact that it is adapted to slip into a masonry fireplace, the insert is built to the same standards as the Alaska Kodiak freestanding wood stoves. The insert comes complete with fireplace closure panel, and the entire unit just slides into place with a minimum of fuss and bother. Everything needed for installation—drill bit, self-tapping screws, white glue, and so on—is provided.

The Kodiak Insert is sturdily and carefully constructed. There is no spot welding; the firebox is fully firebrick lined; the loading door is cast iron. A steel-plate baffle creates double burning of volatiles to produce more heat from less wood and decrease creosote build-up.

If you wish to use the insert as a Franklin—with a view of the open fire—the doors can be opened and the firescreen that comes with the unit put in place. This will, of course, result in diminished heat production, but if the area is cozy, you may want to enjoy the fire for a while. If you want to do this very often, I suggest you order the optional glass doors (the glass is Corning Pyroceram), which will give you a view of the fire without the heat loss. Glass doors do not produce quite so much heat as metal doors, but many homeowners feel that this

slight disadvantage is more than offset by the beauty of the flames.

The Alaska Kodiak Insert comes in two sizes; the larger will heat a 2,500-square-foot area, the smaller a 2,000-square-foot area. They are otherwise identical and both come with a blower, which is installed on the hearth neatly on one side of the unit.

SPECIFICATIONS (smaller of two sizes)

Dimensions: 20⅝″ high × 27½″ wide × 29¾″ deep

Loading door opening: 18½″

Flue pipe size: 8″

Materials: ⁵⁄₁₆″ and ¼″ welded steel, cast-iron doors, firebrick-lined firebox, chrome trim

Shipping weight: 425 lbs.

Heating capacity: 2,000 sq. ft.

Log length: 26″

Warranty: Lifetime limited warranty for original purchaser; 10-year limited warranty on materials, 1-year limited warranty on Fiberglas seal and firebrick, 45-day return privilege

Industry approvals: Tested and approved at Terralab Engineers, Salt Lake City, Utah

Burn time: 8–10 hours

Options: Corning Pyroceram glass doors

Approximate price: $739 with metal doors; $769 with glass doors

American Stovalator Insert

The American Stovalator is an easy-to-install insert that efficiently produces convected heat both without and with a fan blower. Installation time—from uncrating to sliding into the fireplace after sealing with fiberglass gasketing—has taken as little as 30 minutes.

The Stovalator comes in a number of sizes to fit many standard fireplaces and is also available for corner and see-through fireplaces. If your fireplace should not fall into any of the standard sizes, Stovalator will custom design a unit for you.

Large glass doors of Corning Pyrex borosilicate glass make loading and ash removal easier and can be dressed up with optional brass trim. The firebox is constructed of 10-gauge steel and has a poured refractory cement floor and a firebrick lining. This type of material retains heat for a longer period of time than metal and will continue to warm the air even after the fire has died down. Although an optional blower is available, the manufacturer claims a high BTU production through natural convection alone.

Once in place, the Stovalator extends approximately 2 inches beyond the fireplace opening, so a wood mantel within the clearance to combustibles range should be protected by the optional heat shield.

The glass is easily removed for cleaning, and Stovalator has its own glass cleaner, which it highly recommends. An optional grate to keep logs from falling against the glass doors is strongly recommended and will greatly reduce the likelihood of the glass being broken.

SPECIFICATIONS

Dimensions: Various; custom units also available
Materials: 10- and 16-gauge steel, Corning Pyrex borosilicate glass
Shipping weight: 190 lbs., crated
Heating capacity: 37,000 BTU's without fan; 50,000 BTU's with fan
Warranty: 3-year guarantee on workmanship and materials (excluding glass)
Industry approvals: No UL guidelines at this time for inserts
Burn time: 6 hours
Options: Booster fan, log grate, heat shield, brass trim
Approximate price: $475–$505

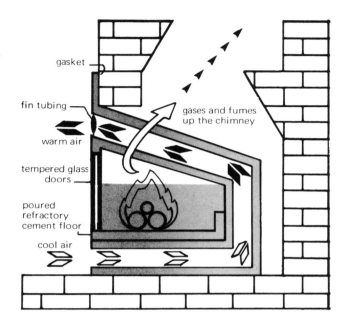

gasket
fin tubing
warm air
tempered glass doors
poured refractory cement floor
cool air
gases and fumes up the chimney

Ashley Combination Coal- and Wood-Burning Circulator 7150 C

Ashley has been making stoves since 1905 and their automatic thermostatically controlled cabinet stoves are one of the best sellers in their field.

The 7150 C is their popular C-60 adapted to burn coal as well as wood. It has a cast-iron, rotating duplex shaker grate, cast-iron brick retainers, and firebrick lining. In addition, it has a special positive pressure relief valve on the loading door to eliminate pressure build-up, which can cause backpuffing. All these features mean that the 7150 C will burn coal safely and efficiently. The installation and operating instructions are quite detailed and tell you many things you may not know, especially about burning coal.

The 7150 C may be used as a freestanding stove, but it is well suited to venting into an existing fireplace because it has a 12-inch clearance to combustibles, instead of the usual 36 inches (but check your local building code). Installation and operation instructions have a special section on fireplace installation, which may be unnecessarily caution-ary but which certainly emphasize safety and an ideal type of installation.

Aside from its coal-burning capability, the Ashley Circulator is similar to the C-60 circulator, both in appearance and in operation. Its automatic thermostatically controlled damper is an easy way to run a fire at any heat level desired. It will hold a fire overnight without any difficulty—or all day, if you are away. There is a very efficient downdraft system, a rotating shaker grate, and a large, convenient ashpan. The cabinet wipes clean with a damp cloth (but let it cool down first) and won't rust. Although the manufacturer cannot give the heating capacity because the stove is now being tested, I think it safe to assume it is at least as efficient as the C-60, which produces a glorious amount of heat and can easily heat a whole house (if other factors are favorable). If you have a large area to heat, order the optional blower. Should you prefer to try the stove without it, it can be added later, with about ten minutes work.

SPECIFICATIONS

Dimensions: 36″ high × 35″ wide × 21″ deep

Firebox size: 21½″ high × 11½″ wide × 24″ long

Loading door opening: 9¾″ × 13⅜″

Flue pipe size: 6″

Materials: Cold-rolled steel, sheet steel, cast iron, firebrick

Shipping weight: 275 lbs.

Heating capacity: Independent testing in progress

Log length: 22″

Warranty: 1-year limited warranty

Industry approvals: UL

Color: Brown with wood grain and silvertone grille

Burn time: 12 hours

Options: Warm floor blower, draft equalizer, stove board

Approximate price: $450–$550

105

Ashley Fireplace Insert

The Ashley Insert is a combination coal- and wood-burning circulator with an automatic thermostatically controlled damper. An automatic thermostat can be a boon to anyone who wants to have wood or coal heat but who must be away for several hours at a time—at work, for instance. Once you learn how to run the stove with the thermostat, you can dial your heat and the stove will respond automatically as long as sufficient fuel is present.

Like most inserts, the Ashley can be installed without any special tools and without any flue work. The manufacturer estimates it will take about three hours from crate to your first warming fire, and provides complete, illustrated instructions that lean over backward to emphasize safety.

The heat produced is a combination of radiant heat from the doors and the part of the body extending beyond the panel covering the fireplace opening, and convective heat created by cool air being drawn in at floor level, heated as it goes around the firebox and sent back into the room from the top and sides. An optional thermostatically controlled blower increases hot air production to 250–300 cubic feet per minute. Unlike some inserts, however, the Ashley will operate efficiently even without the blower.

The doors are individually hand-cast iron. They are easy to remove when you wish to view the open fire, and an optional firescreen is available for that purpose.

The standard model burns wood; a wood grate is optional. If you wish to burn coal, just order the optional coal basket. In any case, the ashpan is a convenient way of taking care of an otherwise slightly awkward chore.

While the Ashley Insert is new in their line, Ashley Thermostatically Controlled Stoves have been made in America for a long time and the company is proud of the fact that it still has replacement parts for stoves that were bought over fifty years ago.

SPECIFICATIONS

Dimensions: 24″ high × 34¾″ wide × 25″ deep (including 7″ hearth)

Firebox size: 18 ⅛″ high × 25¾″ wide × 15⅝″ deep

Loading door size: 24″ × 15″

Materials: ¼″ plate-steel firebox, cast-iron doors and frames, 18-gauge steel surround panel

Shipping weight: 330 lbs.

Heating capacity: Independent testing in progress

Log length: 24″

Warranty: 1-year limited warranty

Industry approvals: Independent testing in progress

Burn time: 12 hours

Options: Air circulation blower, cast-iron grate (wood), cast-iron basket grate (coal), firescreen

Approximate price: $600–$700

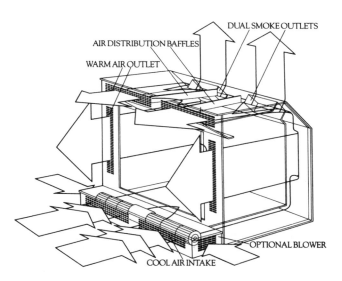

DUAL SMOKE OUTLETS
AIR DISTRIBUTION BAFFLES
WARM AIR OUTLET
OPTIONAL BLOWER
COOL AIR INTAKE

Bell Foundry Grates

The Bell Foundry manufactures heater and boiler burners, as well as fireplace accessories, so you can assume they know how to make durable fireplace grates. Their grates are meant to be used in the fireplace instead of andirons and will produce somewhat more heat.

There are two models to choose from and both will burn coal as well as wood. They are made of cast iron and each has certain special features.

The Old World Grate has an "antique iron" appearance and its design creates a self-stocking fire; as the logs or coals burn, they roll to a low cradle position, which is designed for more complete combustion than if the grate were entirely horizontal. The Old World Grate weighs 45 pounds and is about $12.

The basket grate has removable ends, to accommodate long logs, and the tapered design centers the logs as they burn. It is available in lengths from 15 to 34 inches and weighs from 19 to 32 pounds. The price is approximately $18.

107

Better 'N Ben's #501

In 1974, the University of Connecticut evaluated the original Better 'N Ben's stove as "sturdy, economical, safe, easy to install." Since then, the manufacturer has made improvements and added models so that the original good stove is even better today.

The #501 is somewhat larger than the #101 (the current version of the original), but it has all the desirable features, such as its own fireplace closure panel.

The stove is airtight, with a full baffle system and internal damper (though you will have to point this out to your building inspector). The fire is viewed through a glass panel so that you can enjoy the sight of the flames without the heat loss of an open fire. You might want to order the cast-iron insert that can replace this panel; it's good to have on hand in case the glass breaks (even the best does sometimes) and renders the stove unusable (while you wait for a replacement).

Burn time is approximately 14 hours on one load of wood and the firebox takes a good-sized 22-inch log—a timesaver both in cutting the wood and in frequency of loading.

You don't have to be especially handy to install this stove yourself. Everything is provided except a wrench and possibly a stovepipe elbow. The panel (42 by 34½ inches is standard; other sizes are available but extra) that closes off the fireplace has locking clamps to give you a tight fit, as well as a heat deflector in case you have a wood mantel. The

manufacturer's instructions are clear, simple, and complete, and allow for most contingencies, such as an uneven hearth or a rough fieldstone opening. It takes two hours or less to install.

The door has a non-asbestos gasket and is positive-locking so that a log falling against it won't trip it open. The knob that operates the internal damper stays cool; you don't have to wear gloves to handle it.

Each stove is signed with the initials of the welder who worked on it (one welder per stove), a feature that gives a welder pride in his work and allows the manufacturer to have an instant means of checking for quality control.

SPECIFICATIONS
Firebox size: 19″ high × 19″ wide × 25″ deep
Loading door opening: 10½″ × 13″
Materials: ¼″ carbon-steel plate, full firebrick lining, cast-iron door, non-asbestos gasket, safety glass
Shipping weight: 380 lbs., including panel
Heating capacity: 55,000 BTU's
Log length: 22″
Warranty: 12-month limited warranty on defects and workmanship
Options: Baking oven (see page 109); broiler grill; cast-iron door insert (to use instead of glass panel)
Burn time: 14 hours
Approximate price: $629

108

Better 'N Ben's Baking Oven

Any wood stove with a large enough flat surface is useful for cooking; here is an accessory that adds baking, roasting, and casserole capability—all with heat that is already being produced.

First of all, the oven is completely collapsible, so it is easy to store when not in use. Second, it is designed to be used with stoves in many RV's, so you can take it with you on your trips.

It has two shelves and a glass viewing window that allows you to see how your cake is rising or your roast is browning. The baking thermometer is accurate but should be checked regularly, as should any oven thermometer. Since it is unlikely you will adjust the fire to your cooking temperature needs (as you would with a cook stove), you may want to experiment with ways of controlling the temperature when you need a cooler oven, etc. Cooks have always been ingenious and this presents a comparatively small challenge. The more you use it, the more you will be delighted with this kind of cooking, and it is a lifesaver if you have an electric cook stove and live in an area of frequent power shortages.

SPECIFICATIONS
Dimensions: 11″ high × 12″ wide × 10″ deep
Materials: steel, safety-glass window
Weight: 8 lbs.
Approximate price: $50

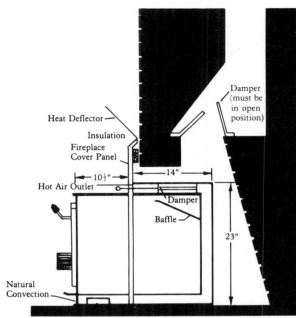

Better 'N Ben's #701 Insert

The important difference between this stove and Better 'N Ben's #501 is that it doesn't extend as far from the fireplace opening into the room. Since it is an insert, most of the stove is behind the panel; only 10½ inches extends past the panel onto the hearth. This is a big help if your room is small or arranged in such a way that having a stove protrude further would be inconvenient. As with all inserts, however, you sacrifice heat production; even with the added convection heat feature, the #701 will not provide as much heat as the #501 unless you purchase an optional blower. The blower will bring heat production up to that of the #501—as long as you have electricity. You have to weigh your own needs in determining which of these stoves would suit you better. Incidentally, the manufacturer says the blower "costs less than a dollar a week" to operate.

Another difference between the two stoves is that the #701 comes with a see-through screen for viewing the fire with the doors open. The view area is considerably larger, but the screen allows heat loss that the glass panel of the #501 prevents. If you are so fond of watching the leaping flames without a glass between you and the fire that you are willing to sacrifice heat, this might be the stove you will prefer, but at least you should be aware of

the trade-off. Of course, as soon as you close the doors, efficient heat production begins again.

The blower increases heat production while it is in operation, but you will not be left completely without heat in the event of a power failure. Natural convection will draw air out of the room, up around the firebox, and out into the room as warm air, so you will still get the benefit of this feature; the difference is that the amount of air circulated without the help of the blower will be much less and will, therefore, warm a smaller area.

SPECIFICATIONS

Firebox size: 18" high × 26" wide × 23" deep
Loading door opening: 18" × 10½"
Materials: ¼" carbon-steel plate, full firebrick lining, cast-iron door, see-through screen door, non-asbestos gasket
Shipping weight: 500 lbs., including panel
Heating capacity: 55,000 BTU's (with blower)
Log length: 24"
Warranty: 12-month limited warranty on defects and workmanship
Industry approvals: UL, BOCA, ICBO
Options: Electric 135 CFM blower, baking oven (see page 109), broiler grill
Approximate price: $699

Cherokee E-Z Insert

The Cherokee Insert slips into your fireplace but enough top surface extends beyond the fireplace opening so that it may be used as a cook top. In addition, an ingenious damper arrangement controls heat outflow in such a way that it can be vented from one side or another (as well as from both simultaneously). This means the cook-top heat can vary from warm to hot, according to your cooking needs. It is the only insert I know of that has this feature.

As you can see from the drawing, another feature is that the firebox slopes away from the loading door. The purpose of this design is not only to prevent burning logs and ashes from falling against (or out of) the loading door, but also to keep the flames from touching the viewing glass. Furthermore, because of the position of the logs, the fire is always kept to the back, which means that maximum heat is directed toward the circulating air as it comes around and over the firebox. The manufacturer claims that due to this design, twenty-eight pounds of white oak logs (the amount of wood shown in the photo) burned nine hours under factory test conditions with 77.5 percent efficiency.

The draft control feeds in combustion air under the fire, which makes it easier to start a fire, and travels along the sloping roof of the firebox to the front for venting into the flue.

The blower is hidden from view, under the front of the firebox, but is easily accessible. The Cherokee can be operated even during a power outage because the location of the blower protects both the motor and wiring from overheating; natural convection continues to cool this area even when the blower is not operational. You will not, of course, realize the same high heat output, but at least you will not have to do without a fire altogether, as you might in a unit with the blower situated in back of the firebox.

Two additional safety features are a reversed locking system, which prevents the loading door from opening accidentally, and firebox design that keeps the outside of the insert only warm to the touch—a feature that might be important if there are children in the house.

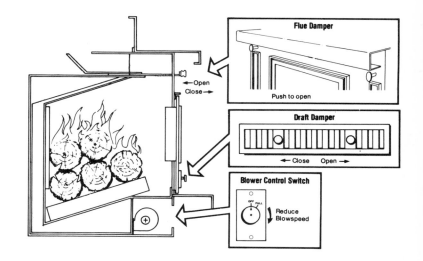

SPECIFICATIONS

Dimensions: 25½"–26½" high × 29½"–35½" wide × 15" deep

Loading door opening: Various

Materials: Highest-grade firebox steel

Shipping weight: Approximately 300–400 lbs.

Heating capacity: 400 cubic ft./min. of over 200-degree-F. air

Log length: 20"–26"

Warranty: Limited 5-year warranty; electrical components guaranteed for 1 year; glass guaranteed for 30 days

Burn time: Up to 14 hours

Options: Special fireplace closure panels, custom-built models

Approximate price: $895 for standard models, $1,000–$1,200 for custom-built models

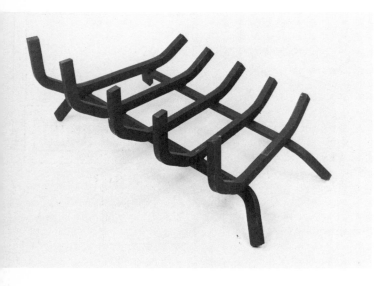

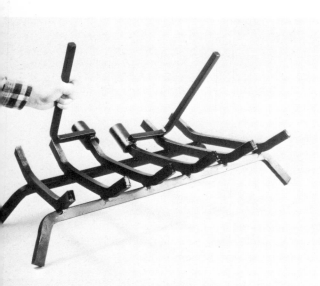

Cumberland Valley Energy System

The Energy System consists of a number of components you can put together any way you please. Cumberland Valley offers so many different ways of improving both the efficiency and the appearance of your fireplace that looking through its line is like choosing from a tray of French pastry (assuming you like French pastry).

Take fireplace grates, for instance. One photograph shows one of the several grates they offer. The second photograph, showing two long vertical bars being attached to the basic grate, illustrates the Heat Booster. The third photograph illustrates the Heat Booster in use, with three logs supported outside and behind the regularly pyramided log arrangement. The Heat Booster slips onto the grate and helps boost the heat output partly by increasing the heat production from the fireback. Like all Cumberland accessories, the grates come in a wide range of sizes to fit just about any fireplace.

In terms of construction materials, the grates are made of hot, rolled, solid-carbon steel, which has a melting point of approximately 2800 degrees F. (cast iron has a melting point of approximately 2200 degrees F.) Furthermore, the grates are built to stand higher off the hearth than usual, which minimizes burn-out due to heat from the coals

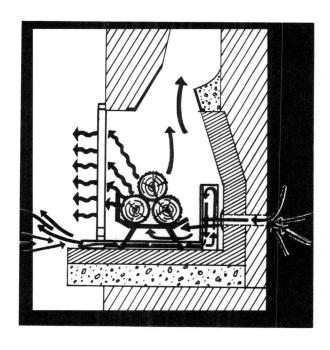

(wood or other fuel) that invariably fall through the grates onto the floor of the fireplace.

When it comes to devices for containing the fire, you have three basic choices: a wire-mesh screen-door unit, a tempered-glass door unit, and a wire-mesh screen curtain.

The installation photograph shows the glass doors, but even here you can take your pick. First of all, you can take the doors shown in the photograph, with plated 22-gauge steel and tempered glass. The doors snap out for cleaning or replacement (in case of breakage, for example). If you wish, you can replace the glass with a black woven-wire-mesh curtain (in the spring and summer, for instance, when you want to view the open fire rather than the fire behind the heat-saving glass). That, however, is not all. For those who prefer, the steel can be solid brass, coated with a baked-on enamel lacquer (the structural parts that don't show are still steel for greater durability), and you can order the brass either antiqued or solid.

If this pleases but doesn't quite satisfy you, consider the Cumberland Bay—glass doors that form a sort of window box effect by extending away from the fireplace opening, with glass on four sides. This is particularly striking on a raised hearth, but before you rush out to buy one, remember that you must still build your fire within the fireplace, so it won't be quite as striking an effect as you may visualize.

All this is intended primarily for winter use, but Cumberland doesn't like to think of you staring at a black fireplace opening all summer, so they offer what they call the Summer Option. This turns your fireplace into an indoor greenhouse; a Hearth Lite fixture (UL approved) that mounts a GE Gro & Sho Bright Stik allows you to use the fireplace as a container garden of greenery.

I could go on and on, but I think that if this interests you, you should simply write the manufacturer and see what it would cost to put together a package that appeals to you. You can add a Heat Exchanger, a Fresh Air Vent, a Blower, and many other items, depending on how much supplemental heat you wish your fireplace to provide. All items can be homeowner installed and none of them—with the possible exception of the air vent—require any special expertise.

113

Elco Fireplace Built-Ins and Inserts

The chief difference between the Elco built-ins and the inserts is the installation. The built-ins are best installed while the house or fireplace chimney is being built; the inserts can be put in an already existing fireplace. Once installed, they look much the same and are equally efficient—a high 55 percent, according to the National Fireplace Institute.

The Elco system of heat production was designed by John Anderson and works exactly the opposite of most systems that use air from outside the house. Most such systems use outside air for combustion and recirculate room air; the Elco system uses already warmed room air for combustion and heats outside air which is then circulated into the house. The thinking behind this type of system is that recirculated air becomes stale and also leads to increased cold air being drawn into the living areas through cracks under windows and door frames, through exhaust fans and electrical outlets. The Elco system, on the contrary, brings in fresh air from the outside, and in doing so creates a "pressurized" interior in which the warm air circulates laterally (rather than rising to the ceiling in the usual fashion), with no more than a 5-degree temperature variation throughout a typical ranch house (which is used as an example because it is traditionally the most difficult kind of house to warm with wood heat); in other words, the entire house becomes a heat-ducting system, almost draft free.

The moving spirit behind this system—which replaces all the air in a 10-by-14-foot room every two minutes—is a small $\frac{1}{15}$ horsepower motor which the manufacturer says uses approximately as much electricity as a 225-watt light bulb.

In the summer, the system can be used to bring in cool night air to replace the warm daytime air that has become trapped indoors.

SPECIFICATIONS: ELCO SLIP-IN (one of two sizes)

Dimensions: 24″ front height, 23″ back height × 28″ front width, 24″ back width × 22″ deep

Firebox size: 24½″ front width, 21″ back width × 16″ deep

Materials: Double-wall heavy steel firebox

Heating capacity: 116,000 BTU's

Log length: 24″

Warranty: Limited 5-year warranty

Industry approvals: UL, ICBO

Burn time: 4 hours with wood; 6 hours with wood/coal combination

Approximate price: $790–$850

Elite Fireplace Insert

The black-and-white photograph doesn't do the Elite justice; it's very attractive, with trim lines, a satiny porcelain finish that comes in charcoal or cranberry, and sleek brass trim. It is decorative without being intrusive. The porcelain finish wipes clean with a damp cloth and will not rust.

The double-walled cabinet provides air space for circulating convective heat and encloses a large firebox and ashpan, which facilitates ash removal without disturbing the fire. There is secondary air intake and an adjustable baffle system as well as an internal damper. The firebox has a cast-iron grate and will hold logs up to 22 inches. To increase heat production, you can order the optional dual multi-speed blower.

The Elite is airtight and will hold a fire overnight without difficulty. The glass viewing panel is easy to clean because the door opens fully or can even be removed and put on a flat surface. A mesh screen helps to protect the glass from damage and instructions are given in the owner's manual for removing the glass in the event of breakage.

Fireplace enclose panels are available to fit fireplaces from 24½" high by 27" wide to 33" high by 51" wide. It has been specifically designed for do-it-yourself installation and the manual provides detailed, fully illustrated, step-by-step instructions.

SPECIFICATIONS

Dimensions: Outside fireplace: 25" high × 31" wide × 9" deep; inside fireplace: 24¼" high × 26 ⅛" wide × 12½" deep

Firebox size: 22¾" × 17⅜"

Loading door opening: 22" × 10"

Materials: Cast-iron grates, screened tempered glass, up to ¼" steel

Weight: 400 lbs.

Log length: 22"

Industry approvals: UL, Mass. Building Code Commission Label

Colors: Cranberry, charcoal

Burn time: 8–12 hours

Options: Single- or dual-speed blower

Approximate price: $795

Encon Ceiling Fan

One of the problems with heat is that it inexorably rises; any device that moves the air at ceiling level and encourages it to circulate in the room is bound to increase heating efficiency.

As wood and coal stoves become increasingly popular, one of the devices that is coming back is the ceiling fan.

Encon has been manufacturing ceiling fans continuously for over forty years. It offers a wide selection of styles, from an antique brass model without a lighting fixture to fans with an assortment of lighting fixtures attached. The lighting fixtures themselves range from a simple globe to a three-shade Victorian. If your décor changes, you can easily change your lighting fixture or remove it entirely.

There are three speed settings: high, medium, and low. (Usually, the low setting is the most useful with wood heat.) All fans come in three sizes: 42-inch, 48-inch, and 58-inch. Aluminum blades are standard, but wood blades are available.

Maintenance-free operation includes self-lubricated ball bearings, 100-percent-copper-wound direct-drive electric motor, sealed cast aluminum motor housing, and a solid steel drive shaft.

The fan, without a lighting fixture, is $139. Lighting fixtures run from $18 to $69. A swag kit (18-inch length) is available for do-it-yourselfers who are not handy with electrical installations or for a room where you may not want to go to the expense of a permanent installation.

117

Esse Dragon

The Esse Dragon is manufactured in Scotland by a company that has been making heating appliances for over 125 years. After the turn of the century, the manufacturer introduced anthracite stoves into Britain (they had already become popular on the Continent) and they have been making them ever since. In 1906, the Smith and Wellstood catalog contained over 100 different "cookers and room heaters." When coal was the most used fuel, Smith and Wellstood stoves could be found everywhere: a country cottage, great railways, and in "ships of the line." Florence Nightingale used a "Plantress" in her hospital at Balaklava, and Scott and Shackleton both used Esses on their expeditions to the Antarctic. I believe they are the oldest continuous manufacturer in the world of anthracite stoves.

The Esse Dragon is a stove from their Victorian Heritage line of stoves; the style is derived from the stoves of that period. It is very decorative, with a gleaming finish that is available in midnight luster and copper luster, both colors are very iridescent. This is not a stove you can put in a corner and quietly ignore; it makes a strong decorative statement wherever it is installed.

Do not be misled, however, by its decorative exterior; the Esse is a workhorse, knowledgeably designed to do its job well. Building and adding to the fire is made easier by both front-loading doors and a side-loading door.

The viewing windows on the front doors are made of mica, that excellent mineral used by the Victorians instead of glass. It is not fragile and will not present the breakage problems of even tempered glass. Cleaning it is no problem when you burn coal, and the manufacturer suggests that you eliminate build-up with wood burning by putting a piece of foil over the inside of the mica when starting a wood fire.

The shaker grate is ingeniously designed so that each bar is removable. If you need to replace part of the grate, this is easily done; you will probably never have to get a new one. There is an ashpan under the grate, primary draft controls on the front door. Secondary air comes in unobtrusively under the decorative device on the front of the stove, over the door handles. There is an internal baffle plate and a damper in the back flue outlet.

If you wish to use the Dragon for cooking, the

"fan" is actually a handle by means of which you can remove the decorative cover, revealing a hot plate.

If you do not wish to use it for coal, you can order the wood-burning model, which will accept peat in addition to wood. If you want to use it for domestic hot water, boiler models are also available.

The Esse Dragon can be used as either a freestanding or a fireplace stove. It fits neatly on the hearth. I have not shown it installed because I think the silhouetted photograph gives a clearer indication of its unusual design.

It is presently being tested by the Arnold Greene Laboratories of Massachusetts, and due to the lapse of time between the writing of a book and its publication, will most likely have received that approval by the time you are reading this book; be sure to ask the dealer or look for the label.

SPECIFICATIONS

Dimensions: 31¼" high × 30¼" wide × 22½" deep

Flue pipe size: 5"

Materials: Cast iron, mica

Log length: 16"–18"

Warranty: 1-year guarantee

Industry approvals: In testing, Arnold Greene Laboratories

Colors: Midnight luster, copper luster

Options: Conversion kits (for wood or coal)

Approximate price: $1,150

118

EZ Set Energizer Fireplace

The EZ Set Energizer Fireplace is the top of the line manufactured by the Superior Fireplace Company. It is a zero clearance fireplace (see Chapter 12) and must be installed while the house is being built or when you are constructing a fireplace. Since it does not require masonry construction, the type of do-it-yourselfer who can put up a wing on the house can easily build the chimney and framing necessary to house this type of fireplace.

As you can see by the illustrations, the EZ Set Energizer delivers hot air not only to the room in which it is installed but also, with the aid of ducting, to adjoining rooms and rooms on the floor above. Ducting materials are not included with the unit. The glass door assembly and forced air blowers are optional; I think, however, you should include them in your plans if at all possible.

The Fireplace Institute has rated this unit with a 31 percent to 33 percent efficiency; in other words, it is three times as efficient as an open fireplace. It is UL tested and approved. When in place, it appears to be merely an open fireplace with a screen (which comes with the unit) or with glass doors (optional), and the air ducts are unobtrusive.

If you are interested in this type of unit, write the manufacturer for installation instructions so you can see exactly what is involved. A local builder may have already installed some in homes in your area, in which case he would be a good source of information.

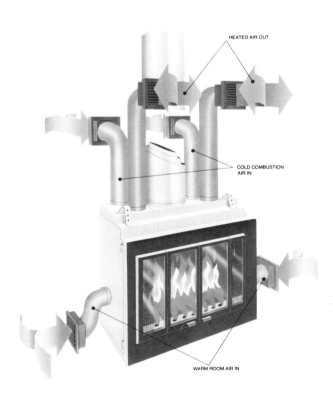

HEATED AIR OUT

COLD COMBUSTION AIR IN

WARM ROOM AIR IN

Fire Rite Fireplace Insert

Once a cover panel has been positioned, the Fire Rite Insert slides into the existing fireplace—an operation that can be performed by any handy homeowner. The manufacturer suggests venting the stove directly into the fireplace, but you may want to use an elbow and stovepipe to vent into the chimney flue—in fact, check with your building inspector, since he may insist on the latter type of installation.

As with most inserts, the radiant heat produced is small compared with the convected heat created by the convection channel that brings air in under the fire, around the firebox, and up over the top, where it is vented into the room through an opening that runs the entire width of the stove. Of the 21½-inch depth, 5½ inches extends beyond the panel onto the hearth; 16 inches is contained within the fireplace proper.

The Fire Rite comes with Tempex glass panels by Pyrex for viewing the fire, but it may be ordered with metal panels if you prefer.

As one would expect from a product that is backed by a 25-year warranty, construction is of good materials—¼-inch steel with a firebrick-lined firebox. The firebox is also baffled, with primary air feeding down to the logs and secondary air coming in to force the volatiles into a longer burn time.

SPECIFICATIONS

Dimensions: 25″ high, with legs; 22″ high, without legs; × 29″ wide × 21½″ deep
Flue pipe size: 8″
Materials: ¼″ steel, Tempex fireglass, firebrick lining
Shipping weight: 300 lbs., crated
Heating capacity: 10,000 cubic feet
Log length: 24″
Warranty: 25-year warranty
Options: Blower
Approximate price: $495

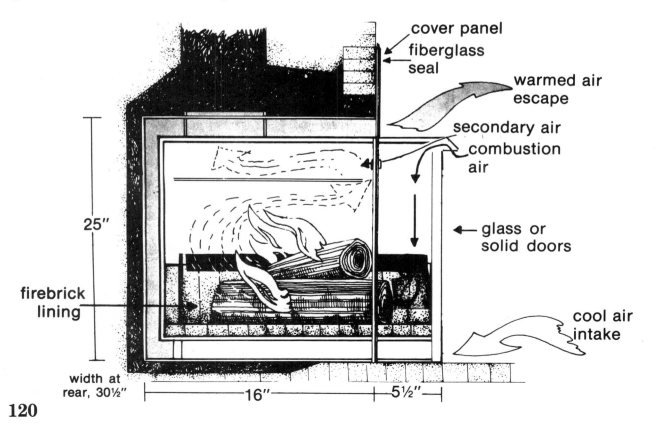

Forester Fireplace Insert Heater

A handsome, brand-new insert by United States Stove Company, a manufacturer who has been making wood-burning stoves since 1869. The Forester comes in two sizes (specifications given are for the larger model) and is engineered for convenience, heat production, and appearance.

The Forester is unusual in several respects. It has a stainless-steel firebox, which the manufacturer claims is forty times as efficient as plate steel in rapid heat transfer. To prove the point, they also state that the maximum BTU production, with blower, can be as high as 135,000 BTU's per hour. In addition, the firebox has a reinforced refractory cement floor.

The glass in the viewing windows is Schott thermal glass ceramic, tested for up to 1300 degrees F., and is presently exclusive with this unit. Both the glass and the doors are completely gasketed with spun silicate (not asbestos), and because of these materials and construction, there is an unusual one-year limited warranty on the glass as well as on the unit. If by any chance the glass should break, it is easily removed and replaced by the homeowner.

The heat deflector shown in the photograph is standard, but both the accessory grate and the blower are optional. I would recommend that you order the grate, since otherwise the fire must be laid directly on the floor of the firebox and this is not conducive to maximum heat production. Whether or not you order the blower depends partly on how much of an area you wish to heat.

The Forester has been deliberately engineered to be manageable for the do-it-yourselfer; total weight is only 245 pounds for the larger model.

SPECIFICATIONS (larger size only)

Dimensions: Fits most standard fireplaces

Materials: 400 Series stainless steel, Schott 1300 degree F. glass ceramic, reinforced refractory cement firebox floor, main front ¼″ plate steel, spun silicate gasketing, solid brass trim

Shipping weight: 245 lbs.

Heating capacity: 135,000 BTU's maximum

Fuel capacity: Holds 54 lbs. of oak

Warranty: 1-year limited warranty on both unit and viewing glass

Burn time: 8 hours

Options: Accessory grate, 160 CFM blower

Approximate price: $550–$650, without blower

The Free Heat Machine

Although the manufacturer is not allowed to say so in his advertising (unlike products in England, which may say "by special appointment to" some member of the royal family), there is no getting around the fact that The Free Heat Machine has been accepted by and installed in the White House —in the President's study, to be exact.

The very least this tells you is that this insert has been tested and approved by independent laboratories—specifically, UL, ICBO, and the Canadian Standards Association—and should therefore satisfy the requirements of any state in the Union.

The principle behind The Free Heat Machine, as with all inserts, is convected heat. Instead of a jacketed firebox with space between the fire chamber and the jacket, however, this insert has twelve 1½-inch C-tubes which act both as a log grate and as heat exchangers. The air is drawn in at the bottom—the part that acts as a grate—circulated behind and up over the fire, and vented into the room as hot air. It has been rated at 38,000 BTU's by an independent laboratory (so you know it is not a claim made by an overenthusiastic manufacturer) and the rating applies only to convected air; radiated heat is not included. Two built-in two-speed blowers ensure steady circulated hot air, and tempered-glass doors keep the fire safe and prevent it

from draining the room of heated air. The C-tubes carry a 5-year warranty against burn-out.

Unlike many inserts, The Free Heat Machine has an easily removable ashpan, which means you don't have to kneel down and reach into the fireplace to shovel out the ashes. There are two variable-speed built-in motors, an adjustable front draft control, and swing-away log retainers to keep logs from falling against the glass doors. When the blowers are operating, the manufacturer states, the insert requires less electrical current than a 150-watt bulb.

In addition to wood, this insert will burn any solid fuel—coal, paper logs, etc.

The Free Heat Machine is easy to install and, because of its construction, not so heavy that you will need much help to slip it into place. The largest unit weighs only 151 pounds. The insert comes in five sizes and will fit most fireplaces; extension panels are available if the size of your fireplace should require them.

The Free Heat Machine has an attractive appearance with a black "leather"-etched finish and "antique brass" accents.

The manufacturer claims that The Free Heat Machine is "far more efficient than any competing machine now on the market," and substantiates this claim with reference to its cubic-feet-per-minute heat output and BTU rating, as certified by independent laboratories.

SPECIFICATIONS

Dimensions: 49" wide, 27"–32" high (varies with model size)

Firebox size: Minimum 23" × 18¾" deep × 13" high to maximum 23" × 22¼" deep × 18" high

Loading door opening: 38" wide × 12"–16" high (varies with model)

Flue pipe size: No flue provided; uses chimney

Materials: 18-gauge steel, tempered glass

Shipping weight: 139–151 lbs., depending on model

Heating capacity: 38,000 BTU's, not including radiated heat

Warranty: 5-year warranty on heat-exchanger tubes, one year on console

Industry approvals: UL, ICBO, CSA

Options: Extension panels to fit fireplace openings up to 36" high × 55" wide

Approximate price: $550–$600

Frontier Fireplace Insert

This insert comes with the panel already attached; the whole unit slides right into the fireplace, without any structural alterations. The insert fits flush against the fireplace so you have practically no part of the stove sticking out in front.

There are several unique features in the Frontier Insert construction. The firebox is bottomless; it sits directly on the firebrick of your fireplace. Since many fireplaces have an ash-removal outlet, you can use that or you can remove the ashes in the conventional manner by shoveling them out.

It has a four-point draft system. In addition to the two draft controls on the doors, there are draft controls on the sides of the insert, below the ash shelf. If the ¼-inch steel heat exchanger tubes within the firebox are used as grates and the fire is built on them, the side draft controls bring primary air in beneath the fire and the door controls

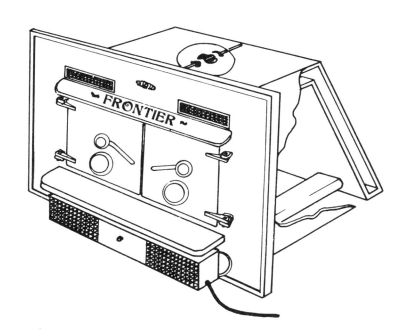

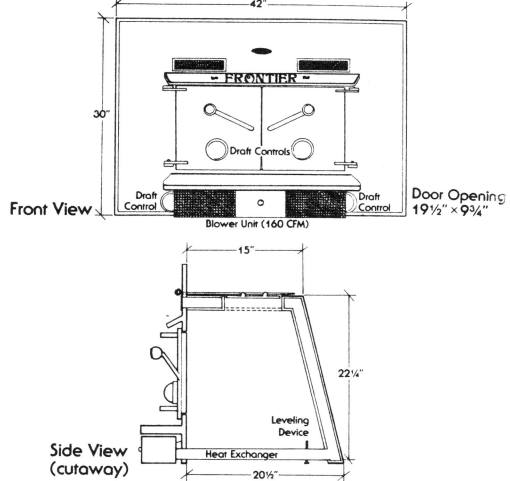

Front View

30"

42"

Draft Controls

Draft Control

Draft Control

Blower Unit (160 CFM)

Door Opening 19½" × 9¾"

Side View (cutaway)

15"

22¼"

Leveling Device

Heat Exchanger

20½"

Frontier Fireplace Insert (*continued*)

then are used to bring in secondary air. This type of system results in very complete and efficient combustion. Additional control is available with a built-in damper that is operated by a control knob set between the hot air vents, above the nameplate.

The heat exchanger works with two variable-speed 80 CFM blowers that are set in front of the stove (where they will not burn out from radiated heat) and the air is circulated along the bottom of the firebox, up the back and over the fire; it enters the room through two screened vents.

The panel will fit most fireplace openings and custom orders will be filled in the event of a special problem. A black safety screen comes with the insert for viewing the open fire in the Franklin mode.

SPECIFICATIONS

Dimensions: 30¼″ face height × 42½″ face width; 23¼″ box height × 25″ box width × 20½″ bottom box depth and 15″ top box depth

Firebox size: 25″ × 20½″

Loading door opening: 19½″ × 9¾″

Flue pipe size: 8″

Materials: ¼″ and ⁵⁄₁₆″ mild plate steel

Shipping weight: 295 lbs., crated

Heating capacity: 1500 sq. ft.

Log length: 24″

Warranty: 5-year limited warranty

Industry approvals: Pending ICBO

Burn time: 8–12 hours

Approximate price: $789

Garrison Fireplace Stove

The Garrison is a pleasantly shaped octagonal airtight that turns into a Franklin when you open the doors and put the spark-guard screen in place. It is low enough to be set somewhat within the fireplace, though you should leave as much as possible extended onto the hearth, both for maximum heat production and so that you can use the top for cooking.

The octagonal shape, though decorative, is designed for increased strength (like bees' honeycomb cells). Other functional features are a brass key handle that is removable, and therefore childproof, an interior baffle system, and a specially placed pair of draft controls. Draft controls are most commonly found in the front, but in the Garrison they sit high up toward the back of the stove. This brings the air in above the fire, which then draws it down and causes the wood to burn from

the back to the front. According to the theory inherent in this feature, the heat is thus directed toward the center and the front of the stove—where people are—rather than toward the back. Another result of this design is that one rebuilds or adds to the fire by raking the glowing coals to the back, rather than to the front as in many stoves, and this reduces the danger of hot coals' falling onto the floor in front of the stove.

A base heat shield on the outside bottom of the stove reduces the amount of heat radiated to the floor and is an added safety feature.

The stove's flat top is excellent for cooking and an optional soapstone griddle (shown in photograph) makes an even finer cooking surface. Pancakes, bacon, cheese sandwiches, and similar foods can be prepared directly on the griddle, which is removable for easy cleaning. It also increases the

125

Garrison Fireplace Stove (continued)

heat production of the stove, since soapstone, though slow to heat, retains heat long after other materials have cooled off.

Garrison stoves come in three sizes, with heights of 29½, 25½, and 21½ inches; the other dimensions also vary, as does the firebox capacity, so check out all three to determine which is right for your situation.

SPECIFICATIONS (Garrison One only)
Dimensions: 29½″ high × 32″ wide × 21″ deep
Cooking surface: 3.55 sq. ft.
Loading door opening: 12″ × 20″
Flue pipe size: 8″
Materials: cast-iron doors, removable brass handle, ¼″ hot rolled steel, 22-gauge base heat shield
Weight: 390 lbs.
Heating capacity: 10,000 cubic ft.
Log length: 24″
Warranty: 20-year guarantee
Industry approvals: UL
Burn time: 12 hours
Options: Cast-iron warming plate, soapstone griddle, firetools
Approximate price: $398

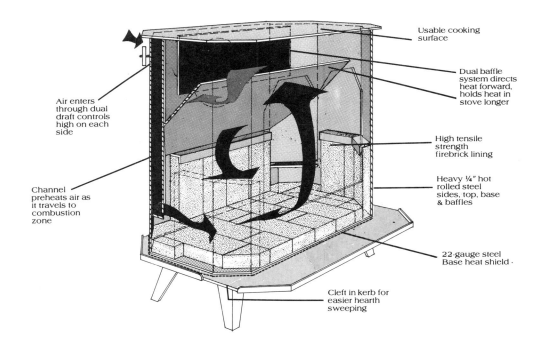

Usable cooking surface

Dual baffle system directs heat forward, holds heat in stove longer

High tensile strength firebrick lining

Heavy ¼″ hot rolled steel sides, top, base & baffles

22-gauge steel Base heat shield

Cleft in kerb for easier hearth sweeping

Air enters through dual draft controls high on each side

Channel preheats air as it travels to combustion zone

Hearth-Aid and Hearth-Aid II Heat Exchanger

The Hearth-Aid is a stainless-steel heat exchanger that fits into the top of an existing fireplace to increase its heat production by the addition of convected air. It can be installed by the homeowner. The Hearth-Aid II is the same unit plus the addition of a frame and glass doors, as shown in the photograph and drawing. The fireplace could still be operated as an open fire (behind a wire mesh screen that is furnished with the unit) and the glass doors could be closed when the fire is being allowed to die down, thus preventing warm air from escaping from the room and up the chimney.

The heat exchanger draws room air through the tube and over the fire, where it is heated to over 200 degrees F. A 150 CFM blower forces the heated air back into the room at a maximum rate of 120 cubic feet per minute (airflow is adjustable). The blower is thermostatically controlled so that it operates only when activated by the heat of the fire; when there is no fire, the fan turns off automatically.

Performance tests conducted with the same fireplace (in a room 21 by 15 feet at an outdoor temperature of 31 degrees F.) indicate that both Hearth-Aid and Hearth-Aid II (with doors open) increase the efficiency of a standard fireplace five times.

The heat exchanger comes completely assembled. There is a full 5-year warranty against burn-out. Glass doors are bifold and open fully.

SPECIFICATIONS (Hearth-Aid and Hearth-Aid II)

Dimensions: Can be constructed to fit about 90% of existing fireplaces

Materials: Hearth-Aid is stainless steel; door, tempered glass; wire-mesh spark screen

Shipping weight: Hearth-Aid, 81 lbs.; Hearth-Aid II, 331 lbs.

Heating capacity: 20,000 plus BTU's

Warranty: Heat exchanger, full 5-year warranty against tube burn-out; parts, 1 year; 30-day money-back policy

Colors: Hearth-Aid II: two finishes—black and brass or antique gold

Options: 12-volt blower attachment (in event of power failures); stainless-steel grate

Approximate price: Hearth-Aid, under $85; Hearth-Aid II, under $270

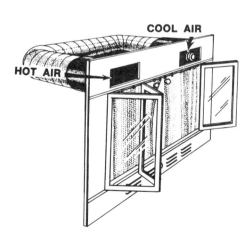

Hearth-Mate Fireplace Stove

A sturdy stove made of low-carbon steel with a rugged cast-iron door, the Hearth-Mate sits snugly against its fireplace cover, which is part of its installation, and protects your mantel with a heat shield.

As with a few other stoves of this type, the manufacturer stresses ease of installation because the cover panel fits so tightly it is not necessary to use stovepipe; the stove can be vented directly into the fireplace proper. If you are considering this type of installation, take a minute to read the section in Chapter 13 on venting directly into the fireplace.

The flat top of the Hearth-Mate is suitable for cooking, and an optional baking oven is offered, so you can even make bread, roasts, pies, and other foods that would not lend themselves to stovetop cookery. Since you can do all this without using additional fuel—you have the fire going for heat anyway—you can increase your fuel savings appreciably. Cooking with wood is fun and is becoming increasingly popular, so be sure to try it when you have a stove that makes it possible. At the very least, you can keep the coffee hot or the kettle just below the boil—though you may need a heat tamer to do so.

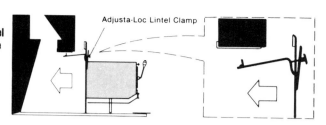

Position stove with cover panel against the face of the fireplace with Adjusta-Loc™ Lintel Clamps loosely in place.

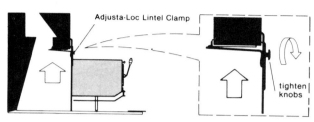

Slide the lintel clamps up so that they grip the lintel. Lock into place with tightening knobs.

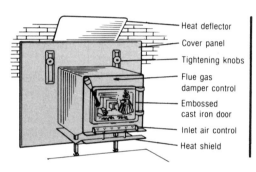

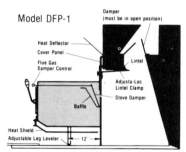

SPECIFICATIONS

Dimensions: 18″ × 18″ × 24″ deep

Firebox size: same as stove size

Loading door opening: 9″ × 13″

Materials: Low-carbon steel, cast-iron door, brass

Shipping weight: 165 lbs.

Heating capacity: 40,000 BTU's plus

Log length: 22″

Warranty: 1 year

Industry approvals: UL; Arnold Greene Testing Laboratories; accepted by State of Massachusetts

Burn time: 8–12 hours

Options: Spark mat, fire tender, baking oven, log carrier, heat gloves, log holder

Approximate price: $397–$422 (depending on size of panel)

Heat-A-Thon Circulator Fireplace Grate

The Heat-A-Thon is a heat-exchanger grate with a blower. It can be retrofitted in an existing fireplace, or built in (in which case it should be ordered and given to the contractor before fireplace construction has started). It is available for all types of fireplaces—one-sided, corner, and see-through. If you are considering the built-in, you will also want to consider the outside air combustion kit, which draws air from outdoors for heating and circulating, thus eliminating drafts that may arise from use of room air for this purpose.

The photograph shows an installation behind glass doors, but the doors are not part of the unit and the grate can just as easily be used in an open fireplace with a firescreen. Look at the line drawing for the design of the grate itself. The grate is made of heavy-duty steel; the tubes have 2-by-3-inch side tubes, 1½-by-1½-inch bottom tubes. The logs rest on the bottom tubes and are contained, to some extent, by a log holder.

Cool air (whether room or outside) is drawn into the fan, fed into the grate tubes, where it is heated, and circulated into the room at approximately floor level. A thermostatic sensor in the firebox turns on the blower when the temperature reaches 140 degrees F. and turns it off when the temperature drops to 120 degrees F. Fan speed is controlled by a rheostat. The manufacturer reports that 350 de-

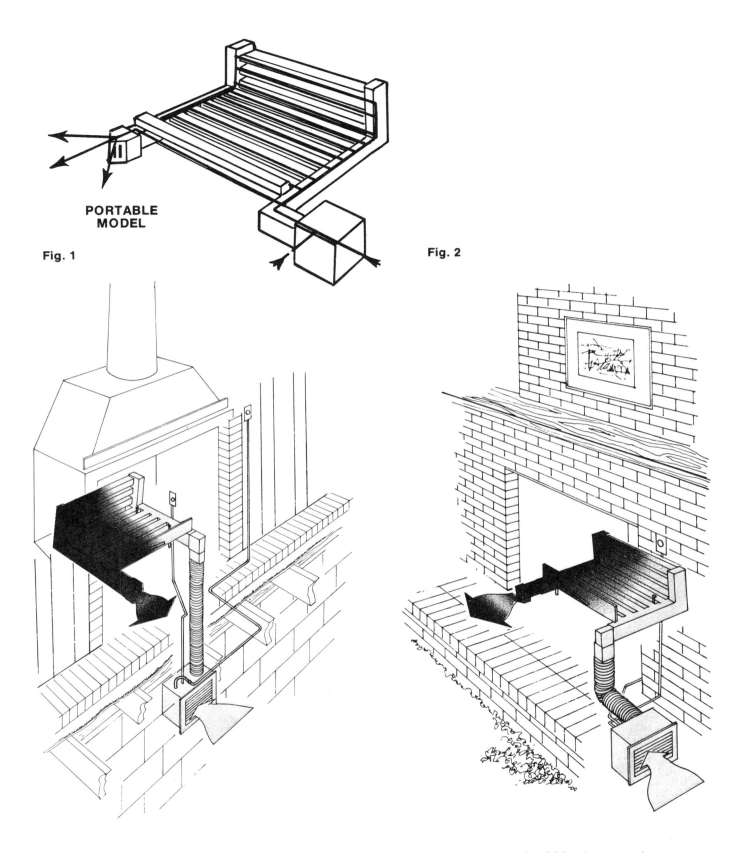

PORTABLE MODEL

Fig. 1

Fig. 2

BBA - Built-in Basement Automatic

BSA - Built-in Side Automatic

131

OPEN-END FIREPLACES

Fig. 3

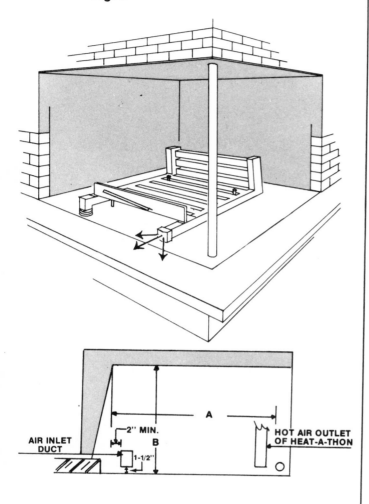

SEE-THROUGH FIREPLACES

Fig. 4

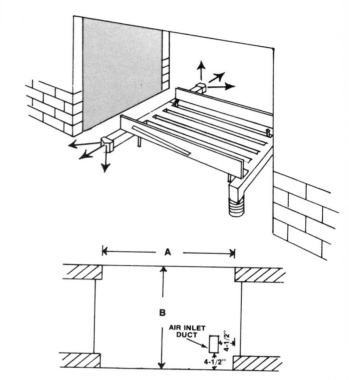

grees F. of heat at 100 cubic feet per minute is produced when the unit is operating.

SPECIFICATIONS

Dimensions: Various

Materials: 11-gauge tubular steel, cast-aluminum blower housing

Heating capacity: 43,500 BTU's

Warranty: Limited 5-year warranty; limited extended 10-year warranty

Options: Upward hot air outlet, right or left hot air outlet, 2-way hot air outlet, auxiliary blower, outside air combustion kit

Approximate price: Portable, $425–$455; built-in, $435–$465

Heatform Circulating Fireplace

The Heatform has been manufactured by the Superior Fireplace Company for over half a century. It is designed to be installed in a masonry fireplace when the house is being built or remodeled. (It could be installed in an existing fireplace, but you might find the cost of installation prohibitive.) When in place, the Heatform looks like a standard fireplace, except for the air-circulation grilles, which can be styled in a number of ways and do not detract from the appearance. The outside of the fireplace is not otherwise affected and can be colonial, modern, or whatever style you please.

Basically, the Heatform is a steel unit with a double-wall construction, and is ribbed around the firebox. As you can see from the photograph, cool air inlets are on the side and are ducted to outside air—the Superior Outside Combustion Air Kit is ideal for this purpose—so that it does not draw room air, and does not, therefore, create as much of a draft as convection systems that utilize room air.

Energy efficiency is rated at four times that of a standard fireplace. Since the Heatform has been in production for so many years, it may well be possible to discover a homeowner in your area who has installed one. If so, you could ask to look at it, and perhaps even see for yourself how much heat it produces.

There are all sorts of optional items available—for barbecuing, for instance—but the one I would definitely not pass up is the fuel grate, which comes in four sizes. A fuel grate not only gives you a more efficient fire (in terms of heat production), and simplifies ash removal; it also extends the life of the firebox: the manufacturer states that it is "almost impossible" to burn out the firebox if the high back grate is used, because it prevents burning logs from touching the back wall. Needless to say, this will work only if you build a sensible fire; the homeowner who overloads his fireplace may find that he can burn out even a masonry fireback.

Any fireplace fuel can be used in this grate—wood, coal, etc.

All units have ICBO approval. There is a 20-year limited warranty on parts, a 10-year warranty on labor.

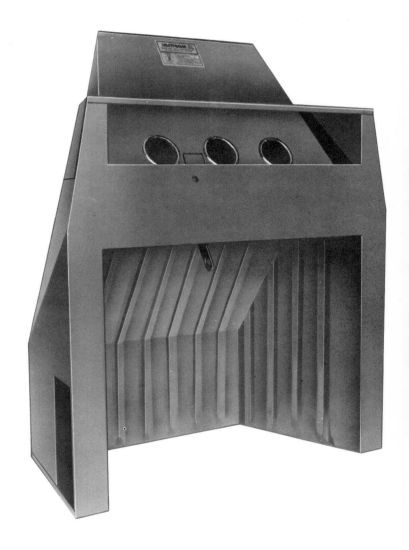

Heatform Circulating Fireplace (*continued*)

SPECIFICATIONS

Dimensions: Various; 13 sizes, 3 different styles, including one for corner fireplaces

Materials: Steel firebox (as illustrated)

Shipping weight: 168–411 lbs., depending on model

Heating capacity: 4 times as much as standard fireplace (over 40% efficiency)

Warranty: 20-year limited warranty

Industry approvals: ICBO

Options: Fuel grates, air grilles and registers, electric fan grilles

Approximate price: $244–$1,121

1.

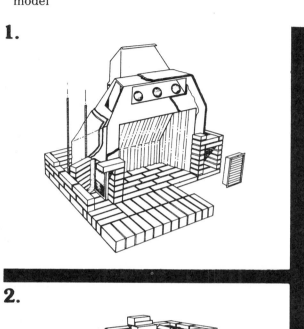

2.

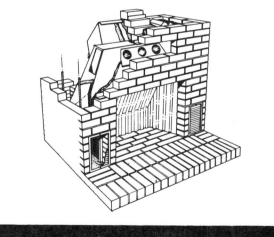

3.

4.

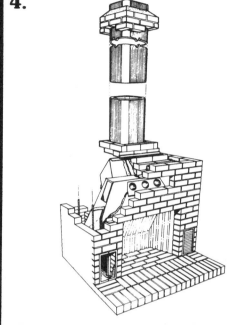

5.

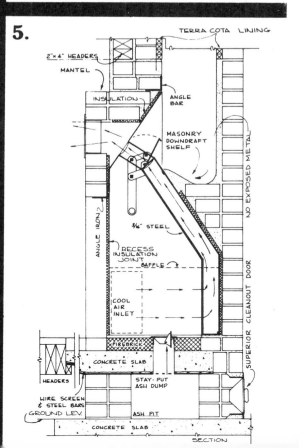

The Hot One by Energy Savers

The Hot One is described by the manufacturer as "a wood-burning forced air fireplace furnace." It is a built-in and is said to produce 200,000 BTU's, enough to warm your whole house by ducting the heated air to ceiling registers.

The unit comes complete with the glass doors (with screen) shown in the photograph and with all the basic components. For maximum heat output, however, you will also need the optional blower "air handling package," and you would probably be well advised to get the Hearth-Air, which will duct outside air into the firebox.

This is not an installation job for a do-it-yourselfer who isn't handy with bricks and mortar, but one who is could reduce the payback period considerably. If you are building a home or remodeling, you should certainly consider installing this type of unit or some similar heat-producing device instead of a standard open fireplace.

When considering a built-in, I would suggest you look at and compare installation instructions and go over them with whoever is going to do the work.

SPECIFICATIONS

Dimensions: Various
Firebox size: 37" × 23"
Loading door opening: 12" × 12"
Materials: 3/16" steel, viewing glass
Weight: 500 lbs.
Heating capacity: 200,000 BTU's
Warranty: Limited 20-year warranty
Options: Glass doors, blower, Hearth-Air Outside Air Combustion Kit, thermostat
Approximate price: $1,195, including glass doors, 6-ft. flue section, insulation, and heat exchanger

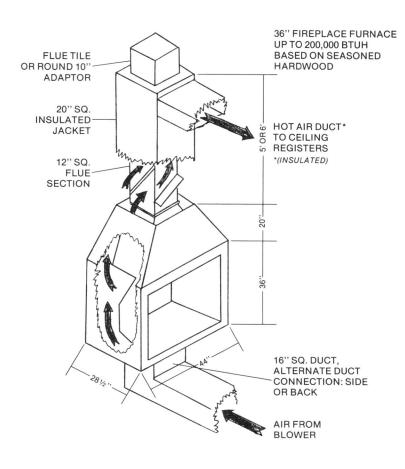

FLUE TILE OR ROUND 10" ADAPTOR

36" FIREPLACE FURNACE UP TO 200,000 BTUH BASED ON SEASONED HARDWOOD

20" SQ. INSULATED JACKET

HOT AIR DUCT* TO CEILING REGISTERS
*(INSULATED)

5' OR 6'

12" SQ. FLUE SECTION

20"

36"

28½"

44"

16" SQ. DUCT, ALTERNATE DUCT CONNECTION: SIDE OR BACK

AIR FROM BLOWER

Hydrohearth

Hydrohearth is one of the Hydroheat heating systems, and like the Hydroplace and the Hydroheat solid fuel boiler, it is much more complicated than the photograph would suggest.

The Hydrohearth replaces andirons or a fireplace grate in that it forms a base for a log fire, but there all resemblance ends. It is also completely unlike the hollow C-tubes that heat by convection and return hot air to the room.

In fact, Hydrohearth is more like a hot-water radiator, except that instead of distributing water heated by your furnace, it does the job of heating water, and sends it to the boiler to be distributed through an existing baseboard heating system. Hydrohearth will work with hot-water systems, forced-air systems, and as backup for solar systems. It will, however, heat only as long as someone is around to replenish the fire with fresh wood; if you spend several days away from home, it would not be satisfactory as the only heat source.

The Hydrohearth heats water like a wood-fire boiler. Water circulates through the tubes that form the grate, preheats your boiler, and is then distributed as usual. This is not an installation job for a do-it-yourselfer; the plumbing installation should be done only by a licensed plumber and/or an experienced heating contractor, and as is the case with all hydronic systems, you should determine ahead of time that the plumber or contractor you are thinking of using is familiar with this type of equipment.

The Hydrohearth must be installed on the main return line and the circulator must be wired for constant circulation and be supplied with a minimum three-gallon-per-minute flow rate.

Since this system should not be operating if you are temporarily without electricity, you should also purchase a Hydroguard, which protects the unit and keeps it operating in the event of a power failure. The Hydroguard is an interesting two-component unit that can draw power from an ordinary car battery. The battery is kept properly charged by being plugged into a wall outlet (through the Hydroguard). If a power failure should occur, the battery will take over and provide approximately 40 hours of electricity. If the power failure should last longer than that, the battery can be replaced with a second battery and the first battery can be put into a car or truck and charged up again. In this way, two batteries—one of which can be your regular car battery—can keep the system functioning indefinitely.

Incidentally, a bonus feature of the Hydroguard is that it not only keeps the Hydrohearth operating but also turns on small-wattage lights throughout the house (if installed to do so), so that you need not ever be completely in the dark. This is certainly an improvement over candles.

If you wish to turn your fireplace into a central heating unit with a Hydrohearth, you have four sizes to choose from, ranging from 17 to 36 inches. Prices are not high by wood stove standards—from $360 to $595—but be sure to get an estimate on the installation before you commit yourself so that these charges will not come as an unpleasant surprise. As with all installation charges that involve construction changes, it is entirely possible that installation costs will exceed the price of the unit.

The Hydrohearth is for existing fireplaces. If you are building a home or a fireplace, you should look into the Hydroplace instead.

SPECIFICATIONS
Dimensions: Various; 4 sizes available, from 17" to 36".

Materials: 3/16" low-carbon angle-iron manifolds; 3/4" schedule 40 black steel pipe grates; 1¼" schedule 40 couplings

Shipping weight: 52–100 lbs.

Heating capacity: 30,000–50,000 BTU's

Warranty: Limited 25-year warranty against burn-out

Industry approvals: Models available that meet requirements of ASME Code and Maine Board Code

Options: Hydroguard, coal basket, ashpan

Approximate price: $360–$595

FORCED AIR OR HEAT PUMP SYSTEM

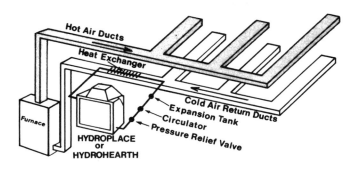

Hot Air Ducts

Heat Exchanger

Cold Air Return Ducts

Furnace

Expansion Tank

Circulator

Pressure Relief Valve

HYDROPLACE
or
HYDROHEARTH

HOT WATER SYSTEM

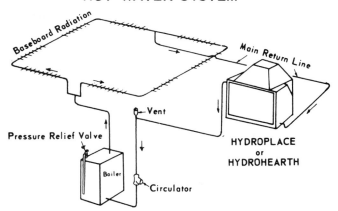

Baseboard Radiation

Main Return Line

Vent

Pressure Relief Valve

Boiler

Circulator

HYDROPLACE
or
HYDROHEARTH

SOLAR HEATING SYSTEM

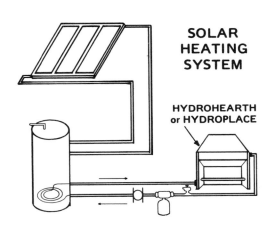

HYDROHEARTH
or HYDROPLACE

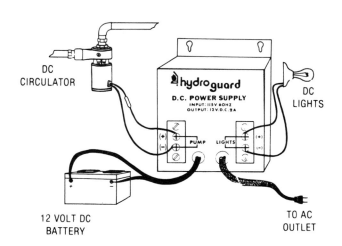

DC CIRCULATOR

hydroguard

D.C. POWER SUPPLY
INPUT: 115V 60HZ
OUTPUT: 12 V. D.C. 2A

PUMP   LIGHTS

DC LIGHTS

12 VOLT DC BATTERY

TO AC OUTLET

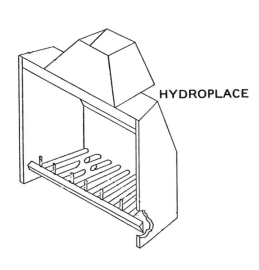

HYDROPLACE

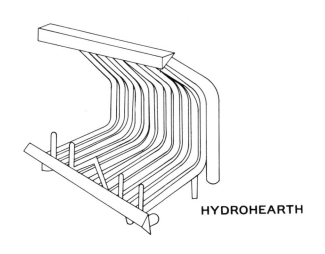

HYDROHEARTH

The Insider

Manufactured by the makers of Thermo-Control wood-burning systems, The Insider has dual blowers, totaling 220 CFM, which draw in room air at floor level and return heated air from louvers at top right and left, just over the doors. The firebox is airtight and delivers an 8-to-10-hour burn so you can easily hold a fire overnight.

The unit slides into an existing fireplace and is comparatively easy for the homeowner to install. The firebox is made of 3/16-inch steel; the outer casing is 14-gauge steel. It will fit almost any existing fireplace; three sizes—30, 34, and 38 inches—are available for fireplaces from 30 to 44 inches in width.

Doors have wire mesh on the outside of the glass panels; this is a safety factor in the event of a cracked glass panel and also makes it less likely that the glass will be scratched or otherwise damaged from the outside. Inside the firebox, log guards serve to prevent burning logs from falling against the glass. Cleaning of the glass is made easier by the fact that the doors may be lifted off the hinges and laid on a flat surface.

At the present time, The Insider burns only wood, but the manufacturer expects to add coal-burning capacity shortly, so inquire of your dealer whether that is yet available.

SPECIFICATIONS (large size)
Dimensions: 23″ high × 38″ wide × 26″ deep (minus closure plates)
Firebox size: 19¼″ × 16½″ × 26″ to 34″ (varies)
Loading door opening: 15⅜″ × 33⅜″
Materials: Firebox 3/16″ steel, outer casing 14-gauge steel, tempered glass, wire mesh screen
Weight: 289 lbs.
Heating capacity: 75,000 BTU's
Log length: 24″ to 32″
Warranty: 1-year limited warranty
Industry approvals: Tested by Arnold Greene Laboratories; accepted by State of Massachusetts, UL, BOCA, etc.
Burn time: 8–10 hours
Approximate price: $849

La Font Hydronic Fireplace Inserts

If you're serious about solar heat, you know you need a backup system. These grates look something like ordinary C-grates in the photograph, but they are much more complicated than you would expect. They can be used as a solar backup system, or with a forced-air or a hot-water system.

With one of these grates, the wood fire of your existing fireplace heats circulating water which feeds into an existing boiler or into an installed series for hydronic heating or solar hydronic heating. It will also heat forced air, utilizing a heat exchanger.

This is not a do-it-yourself project. Installations should be made by a licensed plumber; ascertain that he understands this type of system.

The manufacturer recommends that the grates be used with glass doors (which must be bought elsewhere), although a fireplace screen may be used instead if you are unwilling to give up the crackle and open-fire view of the flames. Without glass doors, the fireplace damper should always be closed when the fireplace is not in use (be sure there is no fire or hot ashes).

The system will not operate in the event of a power failure and if one occurs when it is operating, the fire should immediately be put out.

The grate on the left in the photograph is ST3-10, which is designed for zero clearance fireplaces. The grate on the right, ST2-10, is designed for stone masonry fireplaces.

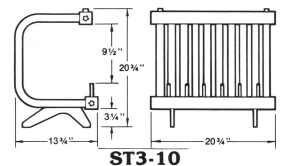

ST3-10
DESIGNED FOR ZERO "0" CLEARANCE FIREPLACES

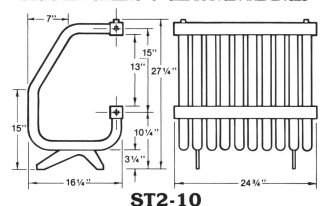

ST2-10
DESIGNED FOR STONE MASONARY FIREPLACES

SPECIFICATIONS (ST2-10)

Dimensions: 27¼" high × 24¾" wide × 16¼" deep

Materials: ³⁄₁₆" steel tubing

Approximate price: $260–$380 (depending on size and model, including ST3-10)

INSTALLATION DIAGRAM

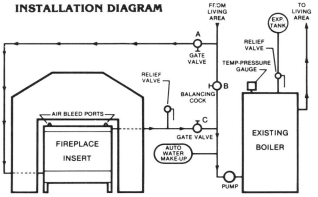

WHEN THE FIREPLACE INSERT IS IN OPERATION, GATE VALVES A & C MUST BE FULLY OPEN AND VALVE B CLOSED.
TO ISOLATE THE INSERT FROM THE REST OF THE HEATING SYSTEM, FULLY OPEN VALVE B AND FULLY CLOSE GATE VALVES A AND C.

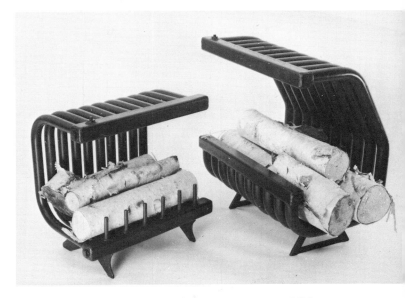

The Leyden Hearth and Husky

The Leyden inserts are quite similar. Both will fit almost any fireplace; both will adapt to shallow fireplaces; both have some of the same options (brass trim, holder panels). Most important of all, both incorporate the same system of convecting heat, although air intake and outlet is slightly different.

The Husky is the newer of the two models and comes with large metal doors (see drawing), which can be opened when you wish to view the fire (see photograph). The Hearth has glass doors, which are not opened unless you are tending the fire.

The Hearth firebox is 11-gauge steel lined with 7-gauge baffles at point of fire. The Husky 11-gauge firebox is meant to be lined with firebrick (which the homeowner must purchase locally).

Although both units are considered excellent heat producers, the 80 CFM blower (said to increase heat output by over 20 percent) is optional with the Leyden Hearth and a standard, built-in component with the Leyden Husky.

The Leyden Hearth is a popular, well-built insert and the new Husky is undoubtedly of equal quality. Both have passed the rigorous testing requirements of the State of Massachusetts.

SPECIFICATIONS (Husky)
Dimensions: 26″ high × 26″ wide
Firebox size: 24″ long
Materials: 7-, 11-, and 16-gauge steel
Shipping weight: 200 lbs., crated
Heating capacity: 50,000 BTU's
Warranty: Limited 2-year warranty
Industry approvals: UL by Arnold Greene Laboratories
Options: Fan, brass trim
Approximate price: $595 plus, depending on shipping costs

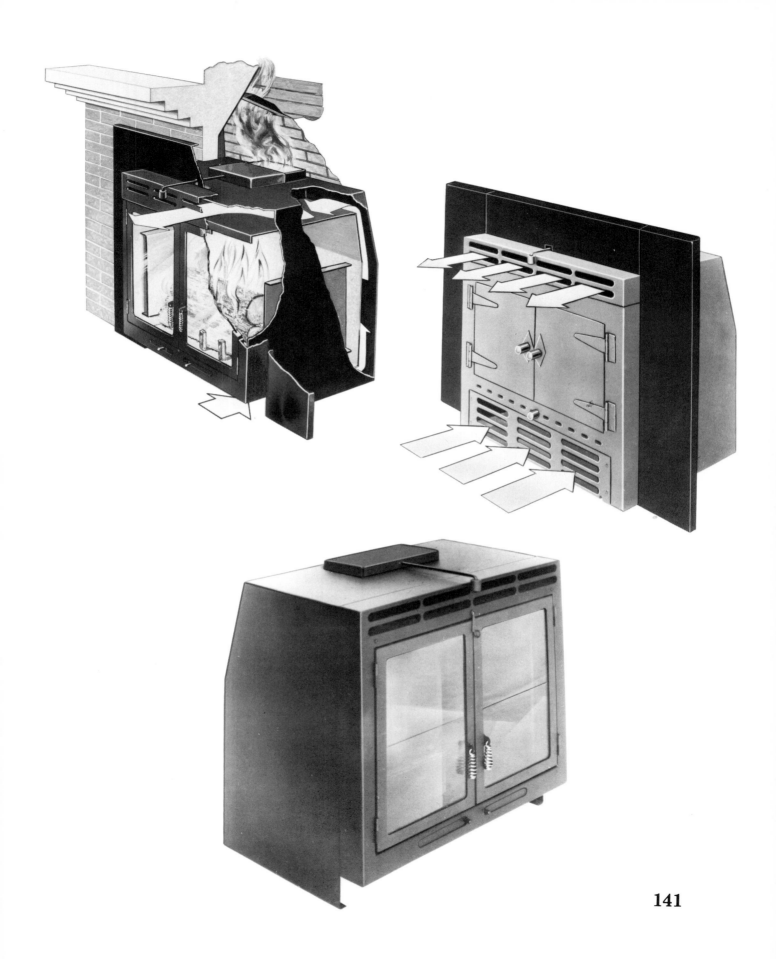

Mohawk Damper Panel

The Mohawk Damper Panel fits just below the fireplace opening to the flue and eliminates the need for a closure panel for the fireplace opening. There are several advantages to this type of installation.

If you are installing a fireplace stove, you can set it somewhat within the fireplace, which means less of the stove sits on the hearth. Of course, this is assuming the stove is low enough to fit into your fireplace.

If you prefer—and have room for—the stove to sit entirely outside the fireplace (a type of installation that will give more heat), it is much easier to get the stove, elbow, and stovepipe in place with the Mohawk Panel than when you also have to maneuver a closure panel in the fireplace opening.

Another feature is that, just as it is easier to install, it is easier to take apart—for cleaning, for the summer, or because something has fallen down the chimney and lodged in the elbow.

The Mohawk Damper Panel will fit 95 percent of existing fireplaces—any flue opening up to 42 inches. It also adapts to any model stove with a 6-inch or 8-inch flue pipe (specify when ordering the panel), and if you have an odd-sized pipe (as with some European stoves), a flue connector can be used to adapt it. Most new stoves that have odd-sized flue openings come with flue adapters that will take a standard American pipe.

The panel comes in a kit that contains just about everything you need to install it, bracket clips, fireproof board, pressure plate, and support legs. All you will need in addition are items usually found in any home—pliers, metal snips, goggles, ruler, etc. Once the panel is in place, the only visible parts are the slender legs and the narrow edge of the white ceramic fiberboard.

The instructions are clear and detailed and take you step by step through the installation. If you can use a ruler, you can install it yourself and save the increasingly high cost of having someone do it for you.

The Mohawk Damper Panel provides an airtight seal, once in place. It has one final advantage—it contains no asbestos (many do-it-yourselfers are using asbestos board to seal off the fireplace opening) and it will not buckle or "suck in," as an asbestos board will sometimes do.

The panel sells for approximately $60.

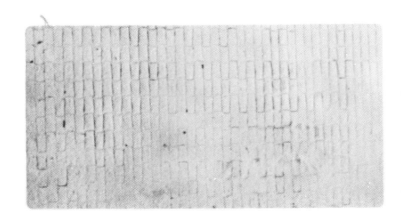

CROSS SECTION VIEWS OF TYPICAL INSTALLATIONS
(damper handles removed)

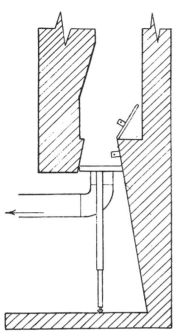

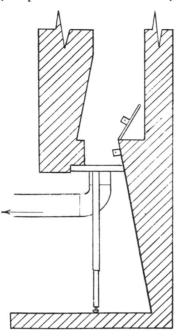

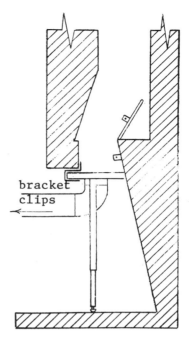

1. Both throat walls slope, very stable.

2. Stepped lintle, very stable.

3. Vertical front throat wall bracket clips necessary to prevent panel from shifting.

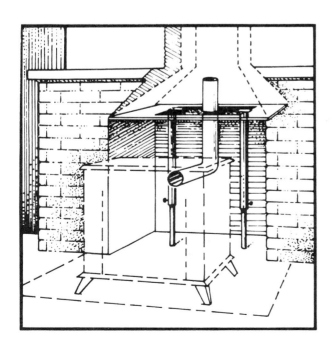

Moravian Fireplace Insert

The Moravian insert retains the charming design of the Moravian parlor stove but has been adapted for those who want a wood stove though they lack the room or the inclination for a freestanding stove. Of the 23¾ inches in depth, 13½ inches are within the fireplace enclosure and only 9¼ inches of the stove extends onto the hearth. The ash shelf adds another 6 inches, which brings the extension well within the average hearth.

To make up for the heat lost through the enclosure of most of the firebox within the fireplace, the insert has a double-wall interior across the bottom, back, and top. This acts as a heat exchanger, taking in room air at the bottom (under the ash shelf) and sending it around the back of the firebox, over the top where it is released as hot air into the room. An optional thermostatically controlled blower (95 CFM) is available and can be added even after the insert has been installed, if you decide you want a higher heat production. The blower system is installed under the ash shelf and concealed by a decorative metal covering.

The decorative archway that surrounds the doors comes in red, blue, or green porcelain enamel (I particularly like the red, which looks like a reflection from the fire), and is a pleasing decorative accent.

The glass doors are Vycor, which has a slightly pebbled finish and is said to be more heat resistant than some of the other glass that is sometimes used, and the doors open wide for easy cleaning. Solid cast-iron doors, instead of glass, are available as an option.

A smaller size is available, but without the blower option.

SPECIFICATIONS

Dimensions: 25″ high × 29″ front width (28¾″ back width)× 22¾″ deep (ash shelf 6″ additional depth)

Firebox size: 17″ × 26″

Loading door opening: 14″ × 17″

Materials: ¼″ and ³⁄₁₆″ plate steel; front doors and decorative areas, cast iron; Vycor glass viewing windows; porcelain enamel arch

Heating capacity: 50,000 BTU's without blower, 60,000 BTU's with blower

Weight: 540 lbs.

Log length: 25″

Warranty: Fully guaranteed against manufacturer's defects

Industry approvals: Arnold Greene Testing Laboratories (meets UL standards); ICBO pending; approved by State of Massachusetts

Colors: Porcelain enamel finish in archway over doors in red, blue, or green

Options: Blower, solid cast-iron doors (instead of glass)

Approximate price: $820

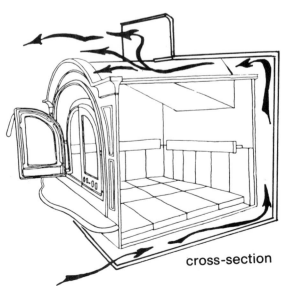

cross-section

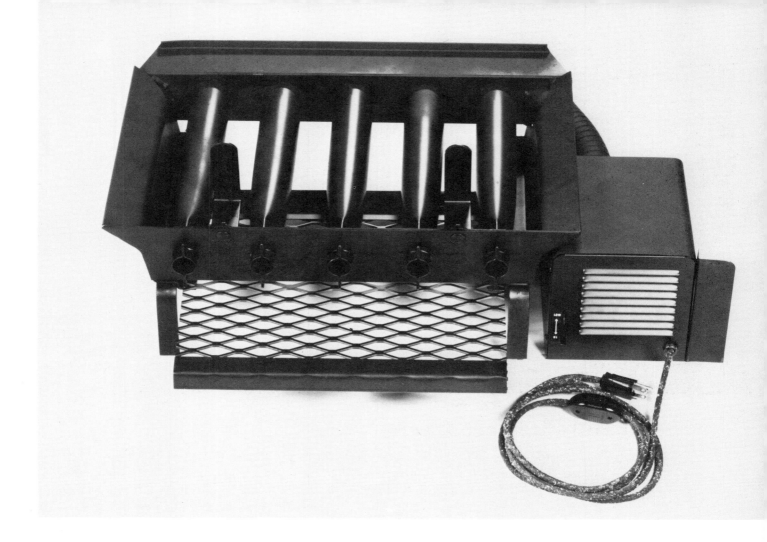

Morton Hearth Furnaces

The Morton Hearth Furnace replaces the andirons in your fireplace with solid steel tubes that not only support the logs but also act as a heat exchanger, blowing convective heat into the room.

There are andirons to prevent the logs from falling forward and a metal mesh grate beneath the heat-exchanger tubes to hold burning coals (wood coals) that fall beneath the tubes. The grate can be manually shaken by drawing it back and forth, and ashes accumulate on the hearth beneath the grate.

This type of fireplace accessory is meant to be used with your present fireplace screen. If used with glass doors, special instructions must be carefully followed to prevent burn-out.

The unit produces up to 40,000 BTU's and should always be operated with the blower. The manufacturer estimates that power consumption is equivalent to a 40-watt light bulb.

The Morton Hearth Furnace should be used only with hardwood; coal, scrap lumber, or similar fuel should not be used. The tubes are warranted for two years, but the manufacturer estimates that they will, on the average, last about three to five years. They are easily replaced by the homeowner, when necessary.

SPECIFICATIONS

Dimensions: 8½″ high × 29½″ wide × 16″, 19″, or 22″ deep

Materials: 14-gauge cold-rolled steel tubes; 11-gauge cold-rolled sheet steel frame; metal mesh grate; 22-gauge cold-rolled steel blower housing

Heating capacity: 40,000 BTU's

Warranty: 2-year factory warranty on tubes and grate assembly; 1-year warranty on blower assembly

Options: Extension tube kits (for positioning blower on hearth), rear andiron kit

Approximate price: $180–$190

145

Old Mill Fireplace Insert

Although the manufacturer calls this an insert, it is really a wood stove that will fit into most fireplace openings. Because of this I feel that calling it an insert doesn't do it justice—especially since you cannot cook on most inserts and this has a good-sized flat top surface that is excellent for cooking. As one user wrote: "We have cooked all our meals—three meals a day—including boiled eggs (or fried), whole-grain cereal, home-made vegetable soup, baked apples, baked potatoes and pan-broiled chicken, fish, even pizza and toast."

Old Mill stoves (the name is borne out by the old mill depicted on the front) come in two models, single-door and double-door. The difference is one of size; the OM-55 is somewhat larger.

Old Mill stoves are firebrick lined (at the factory) at back, sides, and bottom of firebox, baffled, and have an all-welded airtight construction. There is rope seal in the door area and a "supertight" latch that provides a positive tight door seal. The manufacturer's 25-year warranty speaks well for his confidence in the quality of his product.

Both models offer an optional blower top and fan unit. By the way, the round object on the left of the stove in the photograph is *not* the fan—it is a ship's porthole and part of the owner's collection. The fan is concealed in a box and ducted, through a flexible pipe, to the back of the stove. The reason for its position to the side rather than in the back of the stove is that sometimes a fan motor situated in the back will be adversely affected by radiated heat from the stove, and when not in use, may burn out. Putting the fan outside the fireplace protects it from excessive heat.

Both models can be converted to Franklin-type stoves, if you wish to view the open fire, by opening the doors and using the optional firescreen.

SPECIFICATIONS (OM-55 only)

Dimensions: 22¼" high × 25" wide × 28" long (without ashtray); if used with optional blower, add 1¼" to height

Firebox size: 28" × 25"

Loading door opening: 18½" × 11¼"

Flue pipe size: 8"

Materials: ¼" plate throughout, cast-iron doors

Shipping weight: 395–454 lbs. (with blower)

Heating capacity: 2200–2500 sq. ft.

Log length: 27"

Warranty: 25-year limited warranty

Industry approvals: ICBO, BOCA, SBCCI; approved by State of Massachusetts

Burn time: 12 hours plus

Options: Optional blower top, firescreen, trim kits to trim stove cavity out to stove

Approximate price: $466

146

Ol' Hickory In-Fireplace Stove

The quality of construction of Ol' Hickory is probably best indicated by the fact that the manufacturer offers an unusual limited *lifetime* warranty. There aren't many stoves with this long a warranty; all Ol' Hickory stoves carry it.

Ol' Hickory operates with two automatic thermostatically controlled fans that produce hot air through four forced air vents. The in-fireplace stove comes in three sizes—28, 32, and 36 inches—to fit almost any fireplace width. When set on automatic, a minimum temperature of 115 degrees F. will cause the fans to blow continuously. This is the way to run the unit, since the fans should be on whenever there is a fire in the firebox and you should be careful never to unplug the blower when the stove is in use.

Ol' Hickory will burn both wood and any type of coal, but if you wish to burn coal you will have to order the shaker grate that is offered as an option. Wood should be burned on fire dogs that come with the stove, and careful directions as to the best way

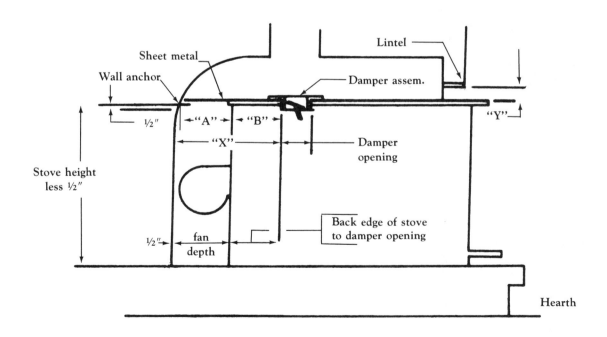

SIDE VIEW OF STOVE
INSTALLED IN FIREPLACE

147

to manage the fire—with an ashbed build-up—are given.

The stove is ¼-inch welded steel throughout except for the door, which is ⅝-inch cast iron. Sliding vents for draft control and a double-wall construction create a highly efficient heat producer. The hot air chamber is not part of the stove proper but consists of three sheet-metal plates installed against the three sides of your fireplace interior. The stove is then slid into the fireplace and the damper assembly installed. This is not difficult for a handy do-it-yourselfer, and the instructions list clearly what tools you require—none of them are exotic or unusual.

If you wish to view the open fire, the stove may be operated as a Franklin (with some loss in heat production) by opening or removing the door and putting the firescreen, which is provided, in place. Even in this mode, heat production will be greater than if you had an open fire in the fireplace, because the stove will still be heating air in the forced-air chamber behind the firebox.

SPECIFICATIONS
Dimensions: 25½″ high × 36″ wide × 16″ deep
Firebox size: 31¼″ × 23″ × 16″
Loading door opening: 19¾″ × 13½″
Materials: ¼″ steel, ⅝″ cast iron
Shipping weight: 405 lbs., uncrated
Heating capacity: 3,000 sq. ft.
Log length: 18″
Warranty: Limited lifetime warranty
Burn time: 12 hours plus
Options: Shaker grate for coal, rheostat for fan
  blower
Approximate price: $859

Phoenix Fireplace Insert

The Phoenix is designed to slide into the average existing fireplace (33-to-56-inch openings) with a minimum of fuss and bother. It is equally easy to take it out if you move and want to take it with you. When the glass panels need cleaning (and eventually all glass panels do), an entire door can be lifted out and put down on a flat surface for easy access. If a glass panel should break, the homeowner needs only a wrench and a screwdriver to install a replacement.

The Phoenix heats room air by drawing it in under the firebox, around through the back, and up over it into the room. This can be done by natural convection or by use of an optional blower that can be fully enclosed in the insert. The fan is UL listed, heavy-duty industrial grade, and blows 320 cubic feet per minute, a considerable increase over the amount of warmed convected air produced without the fan. Because of its position, there is easy access for maintenance (most blower fans should be oiled about every two months), and it can be removed from the unit simply by removing two screws.

Additional features include a sliding exhaust damper control, a wide range of intake adjustments, and back and upper chamber baffles. The doors have adjustable latches so that a tight door seal can be maintained at all times.

The basic unit comes with glass panels, but steel doors are optional, and you have a choice of chrome, brass, or decorator-color trim, all of which are illustrated in the manufacturer's brochure.

The Phoenix burns wood or coal. Wood, cannel, or lignite coal may be placed directly on the floor of the insert. If you wish to burn anthracite, you will need to order a removable coal grate, which is optional.

SPECIFICATIONS

Dimensions: 23⅝″ high × 33⅜″ wide × 22″ deep
Firebox size: 14½″ front height (18″ rear height) × 32″ wide × 19″ deep
Loading door size: 14″ × 28″
Materials: Hot rolled ⅛″–³⁄₁₆″ steel, borosilicate glass
Shipping weight: 415 lbs., crated
Log length: 30″
Warranty: Blower fan, 1 year; steel, 2 years
Industry approvals: ICBO, SBCCI, UL
Options: Blower fan, steel doors, coal grate
Burn time: 8–10 hours
Approximate price: $750–$825

Pine Barren Fireplace Stove

The Pine Barren Fireplace Stove resembles a free-standing stove in that all of it is outside the cover panel, which closes off the fireplace opening. This means that all except the back surface radiates heat just like a freestanding stove and the operation of the stove itself is identical. The cover panel is furnished with the stove, along with fiberglass insulation for a tight fit, and a heat deflector is offered as optional equipment for those who have a wood mantel. If you wish to use the stove as a Franklin, you can order an optional screen for viewing the open fire safely.

The stove is firebrick lined and has a "Scandinavian-type" baffle system as well as secondary draft intake over the top of the door. For even greater heat production, an optional heat exchanger, with blower, is available.

The Pine Barren comes in two sizes (specifications are given for the larger size) and the fireplace closure panels come in four sizes and, in addition, may be custom ordered if necessary. The manufacturer will also make adjustments in the event that you wish to use this unit with a raised hearth.

SPECIFICATIONS (PBF-1)
Dimensions: 22½" high × 18" wide × 26" deep
Loading door opening: 11" × 11½"
Flue pipe size: 6"
Materials: ¼" and ⁵⁄₁₆" steel plate; cast-iron door
Shipping weight: 385 lbs., uncrated
Heating capacity: 2,000 sq. ft.
Log length: 24"
Warranty: 5-year warranty
Industry approvals: ETL Testing Lab
Burn time: 18 hours
Approximate price: $549

Preway Energy Mizer IV Fireplace

The Energy Mizer IV is the top of the line of the Preway zero clearance fireplaces. Preway claims to have been the first of the built-ins to utilize outside air for combustion, and they have a fairly sophisticated system. The flow of outside air is controlled by a barometric dampering system that allows you to close the duct opening when the fireplace is not in use. In addition, there is a built-in flue damper with position control to adjust the amount of air leaving the firebox, and to work with the draft controls for an efficient burn. In case this all sounds as if you would have to be an engineer to run it, using dampers is very simple and anyone who manages the fire will learn the best ways of running it very quickly.

The unit comes standard with sliding glass doors, with antique brass finish metal surrounding the glass. It also includes aluminum air intakes, but the blowers, grates, and triple-wall chimney pipe are optional.

The Preway system allows you to duct the heated air to various parts of the room—toward the sides of the fireplace, for instance—a heat-distribution kit, with custom ducts, being an optional feature.

As with most fireplaces of this type, air is drawn in through the bottom, circulated in a convection chamber around the firebox, and returned to the room from the top (and through the custom ducts, if desired).

This particular model is available in 36-inch firebox width only, but three other Energy Mizer Fire-

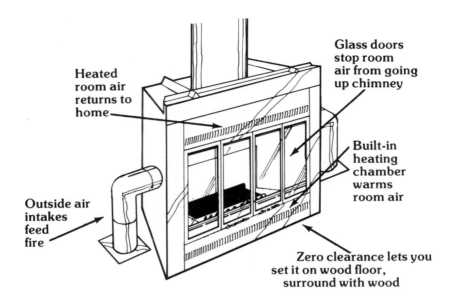

Heated room air returns to home

Glass doors stop room air from going up chimney

Outside air intakes feed fire

Built-in heating chamber warms room air

Zero clearance lets you set it on wood floor, surround with wood

places are also available, and a Preway Fireplace Insert, which offers a choice of adjustable front panels (for various size fireplaces) for masonry fireplaces, will be available in the near future.

SPECIFICATIONS
Dimensions: Various
Firebox size: 36"
Materials: Glass doors, antique brass finish, aluminum air intakes, steel
Weight: 340 lbs.
Industry approvals: UL
Options: Heat-distribution kit, heat circulators, grates, triple-wall chimney in a variety of components
Approximate price: $759

Preway Transaire Fan

Preway's Transaire Fan is designed to move warm air from the room where your stove or insert is located to an adjoining room. It should be installed in an interior wall, and is adjustable to fit walls from 2¼ to 5½ inches thick. It is easily retrofitted by the handy homeowner. When installed, the housing covers all rough edges of the plaster or wallboard opening.

The manufacturer claims the Transaire will move up to 200 cubic feet of air per minute. Operation is manual, by means of a wall switch. Because it is not automatic, it can also be used to cool rooms in the summer through air circulation. This type of device should always be located near the ceiling, where warm air accumulates. If there is room above a doorway, that is an ideal location. It will work most efficiently, also, if directed toward an opposing solid wall; it is best not to have it directed at an opposing doorway.

The housing is a neutral beige enamel; if you wish, you can paint it to match your walls. Suggested retail price is about $87.

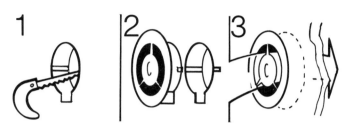

1. Select location about 12″ below ceiling, check for plumbing, wiring, or other obstructions. Cut wall opening 8-5/8″ in diameter using template Form 655 and instructions included.
2. Insert TRANSAIRE section with motor into wall from heat source side after completing electrical connections. (Be sure to check local codes.)
3. Fasten housing on opposite side of wall. Check operation of unit.

Pro-Former-Z Stoves

There's much more to this stove than meets the eye. For instance, the firebox chamber is round—a 360-degree cylinder when the metal door is closed. As a result of this shape, the wood or coal that is placed in the firebox falls naturally into ideal burning position for maximum efficiency.

In addition, there are two draft controls. Primary air comes in through the bottom spin draft; secondary air comes in through the top spin downdraft. The patented downdraft tube extends the full length of the firechamber, injecting oxygen at the top and rear exhaust areas, and forcing the volatiles back to the flame path for more complete combustion. The fine ash residue that results is evidence of the exceptionally complete combustion of this design.

The firebox itself is shrouded in a metal skin, with dead air space between the two so that the outside of the stove stays cool enough to make a 14-inch clearance to combustibles safe—rather than the usual 36 inches.

When additional heat production is desired, you can switch on the unusually large 465 CFM blower system. This system has the capacity to circulate all the air in the average home every 30 minutes, replacing cooled-down room air with warm, convected air. To do this, room air is drawn in below the glass viewing area, heated by being circulated around over the fire, and then recirculated into the room through an outlet over the glass. The heated air is directed down by the design of the venting area and hits the floor about six feet in front of the stove. This system helps to prevent cold floors (although, of course, warm air will still rise to the ceiling shortly after).

In the open position, the Pyrex glass gives a clear view of the fire. When more heat is desired, a metal roll-top door slides down and turns the unit into an airtight. The glass slides out for easy cleaning.

The loading door and door to the ashpan are on the side of the stove, which contribute to its neat appearance (as does the fact that no welds show on the outside surface). No outside welds also make for an easier-to-clean surface.

Care has been taken to ensure that the person running the stove can do everything that needs doing without asbestos mitts. The loading-door handle is wood and never gets hot. A simple tool is provided that will open and close the roll-top door, operate the shaker grate, remove the ash pan, and operate the draft controls. This same tool can also be used as a poker for coal fires.

The Pro-Former-Z comes in three sizes: 24, 28, and 30 inches long. Heat production is 60,000 BTU's, 85,000 BTU's, and 100,000 BTU's, so you should choose the size that is suitable for your area; a stove that is larger than you need may keep the house uncomfortably warm.

SPECIFICATIONS

Dimensions: 25″ high × 30″ long × 32″ deep (with blower)

Firebox size: 19″ diameter by 30″ long

Loading door opening: 10¾″ × 10¾″

Flue pipe size: 7″

Materials: ³⁄₁₆″, ¼″, and ⅛″ steel, Pyrex glass

Shipping weight: 350 lbs., uncrated

Heating capacity: 100,000 BTU's

Log length: 28″

Warranty: 25 years on burn-out; 1 year on blower and parts

Industry approvals: UL.

Burn time: 16–20 hours

Options: Rheostat control switch for blower

Approximate price: $689

Retro-Fire Fireplace Insert

The Retro-Fire insert by Contemporary Stove Works is unique both in styling and in some of its features. Although manufactured in California, where coal is not as readily available as in other parts of the country, this insert will burn both wood and coal. It is possibly the only insert that sits entirely within the fireplace (the manufacturer says it turns the fireplace into a "convective oven"), and is loaded with safety features. For instance, the handles are wood and remain cool to the touch no matter how long the stove has been in use. There is a one-degree variation in the draft holes, which prevents a flashback in case you inadvertently open the door without first adjusting the draft (a common mistake that is made even by experienced wood stove owners). There is a self-locking gravity handle mechanism and, in addition, the door is counterbalanced, so it is virtually impossible that it open accidentally. Safety features of this kind, which help to offset some of the common mistakes made in using wood- and coal-burning stoves, are especially welcome at a time when many consumers with no prior experience with wood heat are installing them.

The Retro-Fire operates without a blower, creating warm air through a natural convection current that is produced solely by the heat of the fire in the firebox.

If you wish to view the open fire, the Retro-Fire can be operated as a Franklin; just lower the door and set up a firescreen which comes with the stove. This will, of course, eliminate much of the heat production, but that you can easily restore by returning to closed, airtight operations.

The manufacturer estimates installation time at 30 to 45 minutes.

SPECIFICATIONS

Dimensions: 23″ high × 24″ wide × 18″ deep
Firebox size: 17″ high × 20½″ wide × 15¾″ deep
Loading door size: 17½″ × 8″
Flue collar: 6″
Materials: ⁵⁄₁₆″, ¼″, and ½″ steel
Net weight: 300 lbs.
Heating capacity: 35,000 BTU's
Log length: 20″
Industry approvals: UL
Burn time: 8–10 hours
Warranty: 5-year warranty
Approximate price: $575 F.O.B. Davis, CA

Russo Coal & Wood Combo

The Russo Combo is designed to be either used in front of the fireplace or set into it. It will burn coal and wood equally well, but to burn coal you need to add the Russo coal basket and shaker grate, which is an option. The viewing window is Corning Vycor glass and is protected by log guards to keep burning logs from falling against it.

The convection air system draws cool air in at the bottom of the stove, heats it by channeling it through the firebox, in sealed tubes, and out through the front vents. The firebox is baffled so that burning volatiles swirl around the tubes and then into a downdraft through the fire for greater heat production. The rate of convected air can be increased by means of an optional blower, but unlike many blower-assisted units, the Russo can be safely and efficiently operated without the blower.

The firebox is fully firebrick lined and there is a built-in damper. A handy ashpan simplifies ash removal.

Russo also makes the GlassView High Heat Series, which can be used the same way as the Combo but is side loaded. It is almost identical in appearance, but is somewhat larger.

Both stoves have a top surface that can be utilized for cooking.

SPECIFICATIONS
Dimensions: 23¼" high × 23¼" wide × 17" deep
Firebox size: Holds 25 lbs. of coal
Flue pipe size: 6"
Materials: ³⁄₁₆" and 10-gauge steel; cast-iron coal basket; Corning Vycor glass window; firebrick-lined firebox
Shipping weight: 210 lbs., uncrated
Heating capacity: 7,500 cubic ft.
Log length: 16"
Warranty: 5-year warranty against burn of steel
Industry approvals: Tested to UL 1482 by Arnold Greene Testing Laboratories
Burn time: 8–18 hours (coal); 6–8 hours (wood)
Options: Cast-iron coal basket and shaker grate, thermostatically controlled blower, cover panel kit, heat shield for wood mantel
Approximate price: $499

Scandia 320

The Scandia 320 is an insert, with most of the fire-box and heating chamber extending into the fire-place opening. It draws room air into a six-foot-long flow chamber, with a 760 CFM UL-listed blower, and forces it into the room through openings on the sides. Unlike the majority of convected inserts, the Scandia has air traveling horizontally around the firebox, rather than being drawn in at floor level and out above the firebox.

The Scandia is baffled and firebrick lined and it has a fully adjustable damper. The part you see is cast iron; the double-wall firebox is ¼-inch steel.

It can be operated as a Franklin, with a view of the open fire; a wire mesh screen comes with the stove for this type of operation. Operating it as a Franklin will cut down somewhat on heat production—there will be a sharp reduction in radiant heat and a somewhat smaller reduction in convected heat—and the position of the door on the right will change the direction in which hot air comes into the room. With the doors closed, however, the stove is airtight and will produce convected heat within 15 minutes of lighting the fire.

Installation is easy and can be done by the homeowner.

SPECIFICATIONS

Dimensions: 24″ high × 32″ wide × 24″ deep
Firebox size: 18″ × 22″ × 21″
Loading door opening: 14″ × 17″
Materials: Cast-iron front, top, sides, ¼″ steel double-wall firebox
Shipping weight: 495 lbs., crated
Heating capacity: Under test now
Log length: 20″
Warranty: 5-year limited warranty
Industry approvals: ICBO, PFS Labs
Approximate price: $820

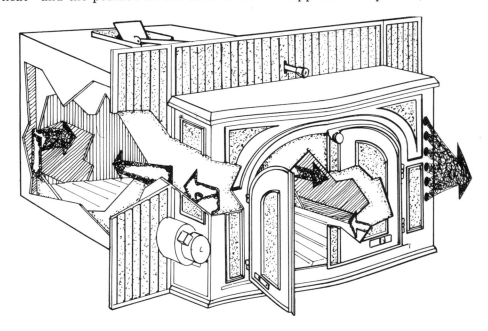

Sierra Hearthstoves

The Sierra Hearthstoves come in two sizes and six models. All are fireplace stoves (rather than inserts) and fit on the hearth against a fireplace closure panel, through which they are vented to the fireplace flue.

The model illustrated is the Classic. It is side-loaded (not all models are) and has the characteristic sloped top that the manufacturer says is designed to allow a larger wood capacity in the firebox and to make for more efficient operation.

Draft controls are on the side-loading door rather than the front. The draft caps are threaded for more precise control. A ceramic rather than asbestos seal helps make the unit airtight.

If you are planning to use the top for cooking, an optional porcelain cook-top cover will make spills easier to clean up; it can be removed, if you prefer, when not in use, but it is rather decorative and you will probably want to leave it in place.

Unlike most fireplace stoves of this type (the Sierra can also be used as a freestanding stove), this unit comes with an optional blower to provide even greater heat production.

SPECIFICATIONS (Model 1000)
Dimensions: 25″ high × 24¾″ wide × 15 ¾″ deep
Firebox size: 19½″ × 11¼″ × 16½″
Loading door opening: 10″ × 11″
Flue pipe size: 6″
Materials: ¼″ and ⁵⁄₁₆″ plate steel; 2900 degree F. firebrick; Vycor viewing glass by Corning; cast-iron loading door.
Shipping weight: 295 lbs., uncrated
Log length: 22½″
Warranty: Limited 5-year warranty
Industry approvals: UL by Arnold Greene Laboratories
Colors: Black, standard; blue, green, brown, optional
Options: Blower, fireplace cover kit (3 sizes), porcelain top cover, special colors, coal grate
Approximate price: $580

Superior Builder Series Fireplaces

The Builder Series are zero clearance fireplaces (see Chapter 12) that do not require any outside ducting. They are circulating fireplaces and are available in four models, some with screens, and some with optional glass doors as well. One model is available for gas heating, which some sections of the country find desirable and inexpensive. They range in price from approximately $368 to $531.

Forced-air kits are optional for two of the models and include two motorized fans (160 CFM) and installation hardware. All the necessary components for installation—flue pipe, firestop spacers, elbows, and termination items, such as flashing or simulated brick chimney housings—are available from the company, and an illustrated price list enables you to estimate the total cost of these materials. This estimate, along with labor estimates (if you do not feel you can do it yourself), enables you to determine the overall cost of installing this type of unit before committing yourself to anything. Instructions are clear and complete, spelling out in detail clearance to combustibles and other pertinent information.

All Builder Series Fireplaces carry a 25-year limited warranty, which attests to the quality of materials and construction. They are UL Listed and Approved.

If you are building a home or planning to put in a new fireplace, you will want to consider this type of fireplace; it is a distinct improvement on the standard open fireplace, and offers supplemental heat throughout a considerable area of the average home.

Superior Outside Combustion Air Kit

The Superior Fireplace Company, manufacturers of zero clearance circulating fireplaces for over sixteen years, feels strongly that using outside air—rather than room air—for combustion greatly improves fireplace performance. The lines are drawn between those heating engineers who believe outside air is important for circulating and those who hold it is more important for combustion, but in both cases, there seems to be agreement that in this type of heating some sort of outside ducting is desirable.

If you should decide that outside air for combustion would improve the performance of your fireplace, you will be happy to hear that Superior has a kit to enable you to do this with any standard masonry fireplace—such as one with glass doors—or with Superior's Heatform or Fire-A-Lator heat-circulating fireplaces. The kit is complete except for the actual duct to the outside, which should be made of brick or sheet metal. As with all outside ducting, your construction cost will be considerably lower if your fireplace is on or very close to an outside wall, but a determined homeowner can install this system from any point in the house.

If you are considering installing this kit, I would advise you to consult the company regarding your particular situation.

SIDE VIEW

Firebrick back or steel liner

Firebox interior

Cast iron floor receptacle

Hearth slab foundation

Firebrick floor

Hearth projection

Air flow from outside

Ash pit

Floor container with dual damper

Foundation slab

Air duct supply line (masonry or metal optional)

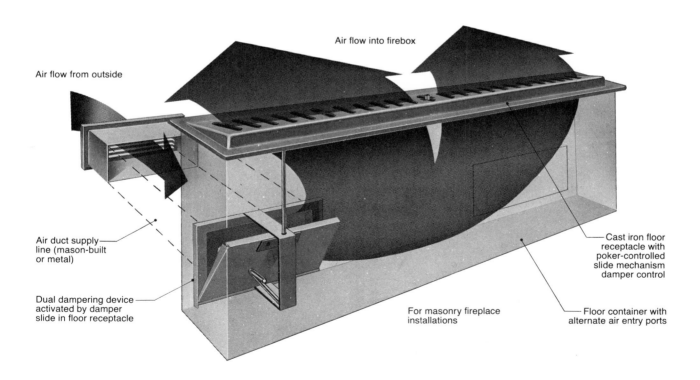

Air flow into firebox

Air flow from outside

Air duct supply
line (mason-built
or metal)

Dual dampering device
activated by damper
slide in floor receptacle

For masonry fireplace
installations

Cast iron floor
receptacle with
poker-controlled
slide mechanism
damper control

Floor container with
alternate air entry ports

161

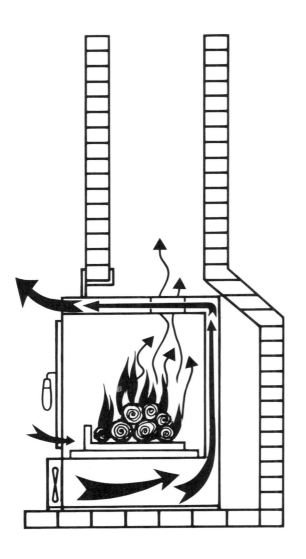

Tamrak Fireplace Heaters

The Tamrak Fireplace Heater slides right into an existing masonry fireplace. Seal it, plug it in (for the fans), and it's ready to go to work for you.

It works primarily on the convection principle, drawing room air under and around the firebox and sending it out as hot air into the house. Two front-mounted variable-speed fans increase the quantity of air heated.

The fire is controlled by draft-opening slides and is visible through tempered-glass doors which keep it from depleting already heated room air. Since glass panels will break, especially under certain operating conditions, steps have been taken to reduce the incidence of this unhappy occurrence. First of all, the logs sit on heavy-duty plate-steel grates fronted with uprights that keep logs from rolling into the doors—a common cause of glass breakage. Brass-trimmed wire mesh provides further protection (from an inadvertent jar from outside, for instance). If, in spite of this precaution, a glass panel should break, the wire mesh screens will act as spark guards, and two metal panels are provided to use as temporary substitutes while the glass panels are being replaced.

In addition to their ICBO acceptance, Tamrak heaters have been tested by Energy Systems, Inc., and rated at 50 percent operating efficiency.

With three sizes to choose from, Tamrak heaters will fit most masonry fireplaces. A decorative canopy hood is available as an optional accessory.

SPECIFICATIONS (RF 3025 only)
Dimensions: 25″ high × 30″ front width, 24″ back width × 19″ deep
Materials: ¼″ steel-plate firebox, 12-gauge outer shell, tempered-glass door panels, heavy-duty plate grates, wood door handles, brass-trimmed wire mesh
Heating capacity: 40,000–50,000 BTU's
Industry approvals: ICBO
Burn time: 6 plus hours
Options: Canopy hood (decorative)
Approximate price: $600

Temco 36″ Built-In Fireplace

The Temco Built-In is a zero clearance fireplace that can be installed and framed directly adjacent to combustible materials. It is meant for people who do not have a standard fireplace and wish to build one with a minimum of fuss, bother, and expense, or for new homes where a fireplace is desired but the homeowner wishes to forgo a masonry fireplace and chimney (although this can be simulated with a built-in).

As with all built-ins, you can use any style of fireplace or facing you desire, but Temco has also gone to the trouble of making the interior look very much like a masonry fireplace. The hearth and back are lined with reinforced aluminate refractory, embossed with a brick pattern, and this may be had on the sides, too, as an option.

The basic package includes all the necessary parts for a complete heat-circulating unit (except the registers, which are optional). These components include: two double-wall heat ducts; two 90-degree double-wall elbows; two insulated inside air vent boxes with mounting brackets; firestop spacer; hearth safety strip.

The unit can be operated without the blower, but a blower kit is available for increased heat production.

For the homeowner who is willing to go to the trouble of installing it, the outside air combustion kit would be a worthwhile investment. As its name indicates, the kit provides for ducting outside air into the firebox, a system that is considered desirable because it eliminates much of the drafts caused by using room air for this purpose. The manufacturer suggests, however, that ducts should not be more than 14 feet long, from firebox to outside wall. The kit, as well as the unit, is UL listed.

The Temco Built-Ins (and there are other models besides the one for which specifications are given)

provide for the heated convective air to be distributed into two different rooms, or all in one room, if you prefer. If you purchase the deflection registers, you can control the amount of air vented into any area, opening or closing the registers according to the volume of heated air you want in that room.

The unit may be had with either a firescreen or with folding glass doors (optional).

SPECIFICATIONS

Dimensions: Minimum of 24″ × 36″ wide × 19″ deep

Materials: Refractory brick-lined hearth and back, painted aluminized steel side panels, solid steel damper linkage

Heating capacity: 30,000–50,000 BTU's

Warranty: Lifetime warranty against smoking and additional 5-year limited warranty

Industry approvals: UL Listed

Options: Refractory brick sides, double deflection registers, standard (always open) registers, forced-air blower kit, Temco Combustion Air Kit, glass doors

Approximate price: $700–$1400

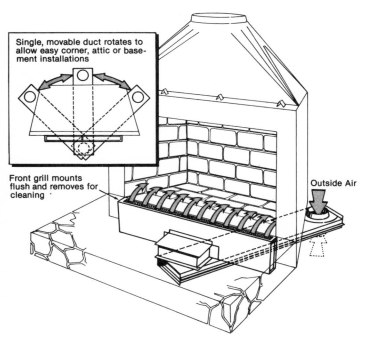

Single, movable duct rotates to allow easy corner, attic or basement installations

Front grill mounts flush and removes for cleaning

Outside Air

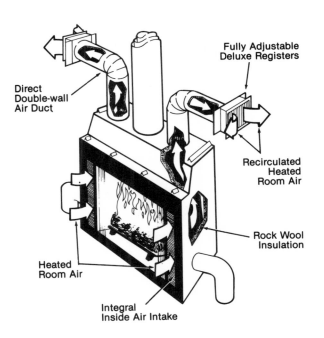

Direct Double-wall Air Duct

Fully Adjustable Deluxe Registers

Recirculated Heated Room Air

Rock Wool Insulation

Heated Room Air

Integral Inside Air Intake

Tempview V

Produced by the makers of the well-known Temp-wood stove, the Tempview operates in a more conventional way (the Tempwood is top-loaded) but shows the same attention to construction detail.

Tempview V can be operated in three modes: with steel doors closed; with doors open and a fire-screen in place; with the steel doors replaced by glass doors. The screen comes with the unit and snaps in as a safety precaution, containing sparks or falling logs. The glass doors are optional but are easy to exchange with the metal doors and, because of this construction feature, are also easy to remove for cleaning.

Heating capacity is rated at 40,000 BTU's but can be stepped up to 65,000 BTU's with the use of an optional blower.

The Tempview will fit into any fireplace opening with a height of at least 25¾". The use of the ingenious Mohawk Damper Panel (see page 142), offered as an option, does not require the homeowner to close off the entire fireplace opening; instead, he can install the elbow and stovepipe right up into the flue opening. With this system, the stove can sit slightly within the fireplace proper and the pipe is easily accessible at all times (for cleaning, etc.).

The large, flat top is an excellent cooking surface; more and more wood stove owners are finding cooking with wood both interesting and economical.

When operated with the steel doors closed, the Tempview is airtight. Its 15-year warranty speaks well for the manufacturer's confidence in his product.

SPECIFICATIONS

Dimensions: 30⅝" high × 33½" wide × 21" deep
Firebox size: 24" × 22" × 8"
Flue pipe size: 8"
Materials: ¼" plate steel, refractory-lined firebox
Shipping weight: 360 lbs., uncrated
Heating capacity: 40,000 BTU's without blower; 65,000 with blower
Log length: 22"
Warranty: 15-year warranty
Industry approvals: UL
Burn time: 8–10 hours
Options: Vycor glass doors, blower
Approximate price: $580

Tempwood II

To paraphrase an old song, "There is nothing like a Tempwood." It works on an entirely different principle from most wood-burning stoves and you have to adjust your thinking even if you are experienced with wood heat.

To start with, you may have trouble finding the loading door, because there isn't one. The stove is top-loading through a removable cast-iron lid (which also serves as a good cooking surface). Secondly, you must build the fire backward. Newspaper and kindling go in last. By this time, if you know your wood stove construction, you realize that Tempwood has succeeded in doing what Ben Franklin was never able to do—it has built a successful downdraft stove. (Ben Franklin tried, but the fire had a tendency to die out.) In the Tempwood, the air feeds into the stove from two draft openings in the top. It meets the hot air and volatiles rising from the fire and creates a "blowtorch effect," forcing them back down to be recirculated through the flames. This makes for an unusually quick-starting fire as well as a long-lasting one, and the excellence of the combustion is indicated by the small amount of ash that accumulates.

This, incidentally, may get you to wondering about ash removal. Since the ash forms on the bottom and the only opening is on the top, Tempwood furnishes a simple long-handled, right-angled shovel to facilitate ash removal. You have to let the fire die down to use it comfortably, but the fire will be easy to build up again, and ash removal isn't necessary as often with the Tempwood as with most stoves—usually about once per cord of wood burned.

Because of its unique design, the Tempwood is an unusually safe stove to operate. When you open the loading lid, increased velocity and negative pressure cause the fire to die down slightly and prevent sparks rising. There is also no way that hot coals or burning logs can fall out. In addition, the downdraft means the stove operates with no release of smoke or fly ash, both of which can mean a lot more housecleaning.

Another model, the Tempwood V, is also available. It is identical in every respect except that it is about 4 inches smaller in all dimensions.

SPECIFICATIONS

Dimensions: 29¼″ high × 28¼″ wide × 18″ deep

Firebox size: 23″ × 11¼″ × 8¾″

Loading door opening: 11″ cast-iron lid (loads from top)

Flue pipe size: 6″

Materials: ⅛″ plate steel, cast-iron lid, refractory liner

Shipping weight: 225 lbs., crated

Thermograte Grate

The manufacturer bills this as "the first tubular fireplace heat exchanger . . . The Original . . ." and it certainly has been around as long as I can remember.

The idea is simple enough once someone has thought of it, and there is no doubt that many heat exchangers now made utilize the C-tube principle of heat convection.

What the Thermograte Grate does is create a log holder in the shape of a C formed with hollow stainless or mild steel tubes. Natural convection draws cool air in through the bottom openings, up around the log fire, and out through the top tubes. You still get all the radiant heat of an open log fire, but you add to it the considerable warming power of the hot air produced by the hollow tubes and by convection. You can even increase hot air quantity by adding an optional blower that draws the air through at a faster rate than natural convections.

A Thermograte without a blower is said to produce about 25,000 BTU's per hour; with a blower, it is claimed that you will enjoy 40,000 BTU's an hour (combined radiant and convective heat).

Prices start at about $65. If you can afford the extra price, the stainless steel will outlast the mild steel and is well worth the extra money.

Thermograte Fireplace Furnace

You won't find the Thermograte sold locally because it is sold only direct to the consumer, shipped from the factory to you. While this might seem a disadvantage in the marketplace, Thermograte hasn't found it so; it has been a popular fireplace heater for many years.

Basically, the Thermograte Fireplace Furnace is a more sophisticated version of its well-known fireplace grate, and although, like the grate, it works efficiently without a blower, with a blower it is said to produce up to 100,000 BTU's.

The heart of the system is the chrome nickel stainless-steel C-tubes that form the heat exchanger. Logs are set directly on the tubes (instead of on andirons); coal can also be used, but it has to be placed in a grate to prevent it from falling between the tubes. If you have an old grate and can take off the legs, use that. Otherwise, order the optional cast-iron grate from Thermograte. In either case, the coal grate is set right on the C-tubes and operated as usual.

In addition to wood and coal, Thermogrates will burn any burnable trash, including branches, lumber scraps, and newspaper. Remember, however, not to make too hot a fire so as not to put stress on the glass doors. It is not necessary to roll newspaper into logs (if you wish to use paper as fuel). Simply put it directly on the hearth, slipping it inside the bottom ash doors. Even a 2-inch-thick stack of newspapers will burn beautifully.

Although the optional blower increases heat production considerably, a blower is not essential to the operation of the unit. You could buy the unit without the blower at first and always add it later if you found you wanted it. The manufacturer claims that this unit will heat an entire home with the blower, but without it would certainly be satisfactory for supplemental heat. It is also recommended as a backup system for solar heat, and as such would be much more economical than an electric backup system.

Ashes are removed by opening the ash doors on

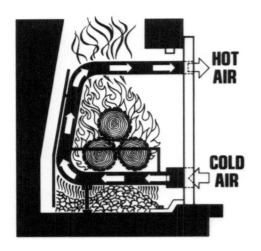

the bottom and using a flat shovel to scoop them off the hearth. Glass doors can be removed for easy cleaning.

Assembly of the unit is not complicated and is designed for the do-it-yourselfer. (The manufacturer claims that an 80-year-old grandmother assembled and installed a unit in one evening.) Instructions are complete and easy to follow. All necessary assembly materials, including a masonry drill bit, are furnished. If you have doubts about your ability to complete an installation, the manufacturer will happily send you the complete owner's manual free, so that you may see how easy it is.

There are 12 sizes and possible adaptations can be made in addition. Units can also be adapted to a see-through fireplace.

SPECIFICATIONS

Dimensions: Various—12 models available

Materials: Chrome nickel stainless-steel heat exchanger tubes, glass doors, hardwood handles and ash door knobs, 16–20-gauge steel, brass door channels and trim, 20-gauge phosphor bronze

Heating capacity: Up to 60,000 BTU's without blower, 100,000 BTU's with blower

Warranty: Tubes guaranteed in original installation for as long as you own your home

Options: Cast-iron coal grate, auxiliary blower, pull screen

Approximate price: $494–$779

Trident Heater Works

The Trident Heater is a freestanding stove that converts to a fireplace stove by the use of an optional back vent. Having the vent in back allows you to use the entire flat top surface for cooking.

The curved firebox is side loaded, but the viewing window is constructed so as to play an important part in the management of the fire. The instructions are clear and simple but should be read, because this stove works differently from any other with which I am familiar. A built-in blower system increases hot air output with a 76 CFM single-speed unit. If you wish to heat a larger area, you would be well advised to order the optional larger blower, which is 140 CFM and has a 3-speed switch. Handles are wood so you won't need asbestos mitts to touch them.

The Trident Heater comes in three sizes. I have given specifications for the largest size, but you may find one of the other sizes better for your fireplace opening.

SPECIFICATIONS

Dimensions: 26½″ high × 27½″ wide × 20″ diameter

Loading door opening: 11½″ × 14″

Flue pipe size: 6″

Materials: ¼″ steel plate on all flat surfaces; 10-gauge steel on curved surfaces, ¼″ tempered glass

Shipping weight: 350 lbs., crated

Log length: 23½″

Warranty: 5-year stove warranty; 1 year on blower, glass, and brick

Industry approvals: UL

Options: Left-hand door, custom leg length, larger blower (140 CFM) with 3-speed switch, back vent (for fireplace)

Approximate price: $610

171

The Virginian Fireplace Insert

The Virginian is an insert, so most of its body is within the fireplace proper, but enough is on the room side of the enclosure panel to give side and top, as well as front, radiant heat and to allow cooking on the top surface. In addition, The Virginian can be operated as an airtight, with the doors closed, or as a Franklin, with them open.

Heat is drawn in under and around the fire and recirculated into the room from side and top openings in the closure panel. When the blower is operating, it will circulate over 8,000 cubic feet of hot air per hour. Even when the fan is not operating, natural convection will be operational and will combine with radiant heat to keep the area comfortably warm.

The firebox receives primary air at log level for initial combustion, and secondary air is brought in at the top and drawn down toward the fire for more complete burning of volatiles. This type of firebox circulation should result in less creosote build-up in the flue and in more efficient use of wood.

SPECIFICATIONS

Dimensions: 24″ high × 33″ wide × 26½″ deep
Firebox size: 28″ × 29″ × 18″
Loading door opening: 21″ × 9¾″
Flue pipe size: 6″
Materials: ¼″ steel, cast iron
Shipping weight: 400 lbs., uncrated
Log length: 27″
Warranty: 5 years on materials and workmanship; 1 year on electric components
Industry approvals: UL pending
Burn time: 8–12 hours
Options: Brass trim
Approximate price: $549

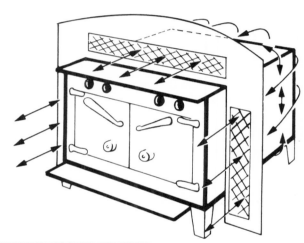

Wells Fireplace Furnace

The Wells Fireplace Furnace, designed by Bill Wells, clearly illustrates the danger in choosing a retrofit or built-in fireplace circulator by appearance alone; there is certainly nothing in the photograph to indicate that this unit can produce 100,000 BTU's (the retrofit) to 150,000 BTU's (the built-in), and hold a log fire for 48 hours. The heat production of this unit is attested to in a KBYU-TV news documentary (which is distributed to Public Broadcasting Systems, so you may have seen it) on energy efficiency. In this film, two Wells Furnaces are shown, in a public demonstration, heating a 5,000-square-foot home in Provo, Utah. The entire home was comfortably heated by these two units, installed in existing masonry fireplaces, and it was all done without blowers.

Bill Wells is aware that the average homeowner is liable to discount these claims as manufacturer's puffs, so he has instituted a unique selling method. All Wells Fireplace Furnaces are sold direct to the consumer, but before you make up your mind you can ask for a "See and Believe" demonstration in an actual home so that you can experience at first hand the efficiency of this sytem.

The most surprising aspect of this unit is that it works so well without ever using a blower. Bill Wells feels that is partly why it works so well; he feels blowers are inefficient and that gravity and natural convection are better heat circulators. From the consumer's standpoint, not having a blower also means quieter operation and a system that works even when the electricity fails.

The Wells Furnace is available both as a retrofit —it installs in existing fireplaces—and as a built-in. It uses outside air, which means it requires ducting, so it has all the advantages of that type of system—including not using stale room air and not creating drafts by drawing on room air.

The Wells Fireplace Furnace will burn almost any kind of solid fuel—wood, wood by-products, and coal. The efficiency of the unit is most clearly indicated by the low ash production; the wood burns so completely that the ash cart needs to be emptied only a few times during the entire winter. Fixed grates dispense the ashes away from the fire, into a tray that covers the bottom of the firebox and is operated by a pull of a knob.

Another desirable feature of the Wells Fireplace Furnace is that it produces five times as much heat as a standard fireplace, using only one third as

173

much wood. Since there is no denying that handling wood is heavy work, the less one has to do it, the better. Also, as the price of wood escalates, using less results in considerable savings.

In order to check out some of the claims made by this unit, I spoke to a family that had installed one in a 2,200-square-foot home. They found that a small Wells Inserta (the retrofit model) heated even "the hard-to-heat areas, the result of alterations and additions to the house. The dining room, which was once the carport and the kitchen area, that is now open to the dining room because of the removal of the wall between them, has always been a cold spot because there is no ducting from the central heating system into that area except for a small outlet in the kitchen area. With the Inserta, these areas are as warm as the rest of the house and are comfortable on the cold nights for the first time. . . . A real bonus is the way the floors are so warm throughout the house."

Both the built-in and the retrofit model come with glass doors and with an adjustable cooking arm for slow-simmering dishes like beans, stew, and pot roasts.

SPECIFICATIONS (Wells Inserta Furnace)
Dimensions: Various, depending on existing fireplace
Materials: 12-gauge inner box, 14-gauge outer wall, ⅛" grate material
Shipping weight: 225–250 lbs., uncrated
Heating capacity: 100,000 BTU's
Warranty: Workmanship unconditionally guaranteed
Burn time: 48 hours
Approximate price: $650

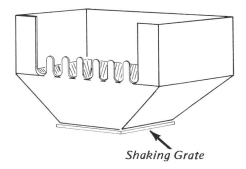

Shaking Grate

Weso Ceramic Tile Stove

The Weso ceramic tile stove is basically a free-standing automatic-thermostat stove that will burn both wood and coal. It can, however, be placed on the hearth, directly in front of the fireplace, and the flue pipe opening is low enough (24½ inches to center) to fit almost any fireplace opening. In addition, the bottom half of the legs may be removed, which will lower the height of the pipe opening by 2 inches.

The design of the Weso makes it especially suitable for the homeowner who wants a stove that will not take up a lot of room space; it is comparatively narrow in depth (19 inches) and width (35 inches), a shape that fits nicely on the average hearth.

Made in West Germany, the Weso is technically a *Kachelofen*—descendent of the great tile stoves of Europe, still in use today in Scandinavia, Holland, Germany, and other European countries. The hand-glazed ceramic tiles of the Weso form three

of its four sides and enclose an airtight cast-iron firebox. The firebox heats the air space between it and the tiles and this heated air is released through an enameled cast-iron grille on the top of the stove. The tiles act as a heat sink, storing up more and more heat, which is given off as radiant heat—so gentle you can touch the tiles without burning yourself, but delightfully warming and cozy.

The front of the stove, between the tiles, has a decorative enameled cast-iron grille that allows you to view the fire through the 10½-by-7¼-inch tempered-glass window, an effect that creates the illusion of an open fire without the loss of heat such a fire would create. Both the tiles and the grilles wipe clean with a damp cloth—this is an exterior that will never rust. Behind the front grille is the door to the firebox, and beneath the firebox door is the door to the ashpan. The ashpan is ingeniously constructed so that pulling it out causes a separate ash tray to automatically swing out at the same

175

.time, thus preventing loose ashes from falling to the floor when you empty the pan.

The cast-iron grille on the top of the stove is a handy surface for slow-cooking or simmering, ideal for stews, long-cooking soups, stockmaking, and keeping a coffeepot or kettle hot. For faster cooking, the grille swings up out of the way and pots and pans can be put directly on the cast-iron surface of the firebox itself. This stove is so effective as a cookstove that in Europe it is sometimes placed right in the kitchen for both heating and cooking. In the event of a power shortage, the dual function of the Weso would make it possible to be very comfortable and well fed.

The Weso tiles are available in a wide range of colors and designs and can be changed if your decorative scheme changes. If a tile should be damaged, it is an easy matter to replace it. Because they are hand-made, no two tiles are ever exactly alike and so, of course, no two stoves will ever look exactly alike; you can be sure yours is unique. The tiles, however, are much more than just decorative. Ceramic tile has twice the heat absorption potential of cast iron and holds the heat longer than any other stove material. It is slower to heat up, but that is no problem because the cast-iron firebox heats up quickly—especially since it does not need a firebrick lining—and warm air is dispersed into the room by natural convection almost as soon as you light the fire. Meanwhile, the tiles gather the heat and are still radiating it long after the fire has died down.

The Weso's automatic thermostat is not bimetallic but is a precision regulator which works through liquid expansion. It allows you to set your fire to produce an even heat level for hours—as when you go out for the day—without worrying about the fire going out.

The stove is DIN approved, which tells you it has been built to strict standards and that it requires less than average clearance. Any DIN-approved stove can be put much closer to combustibles than the usual 36 inches. In the case of the Weso, you can safely allow 8 to 10 inches clearance from the sides and 24 inches from the front. Before installing it this close, however, make sure your building inspector understands that this is safe; not all building codes are up to date. The Weso also has UL approval.

You will enjoy reading the owner's manual; it is very complete and even has a collection of recipes.

SPECIFICATIONS

Dimensions: 33½″ high × 25″ wide × 19″ deep
Firebox size: 18″ × 20″ × 9″
Loading door opening: 12″ × 9″
Flue pipe size: 6″
Materials: Hand-glazed ceramic tile, cast-iron, safety glass
Shipping weight: 440 lbs.
Heating capacity: 30,000 BTU's
Log length: 19″
Warranty: 1 year; 30-day refund policy
Industry approvals: UL, DIN
Burn time: 10 hours (wood); 24 hours (coal)
Tile colors: Burnished tan, satin jade, satin bronze, burgundy, bottle green
Approximate price: $1,175

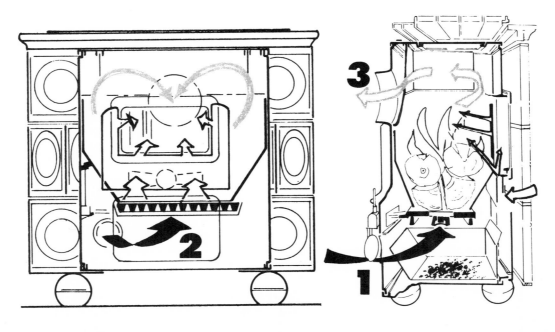

Names and Addresses of Manufacturers

Aeroheator Company
P.O. Box 1461
Springfield, Virginia 22151

Alaska Kodiak Woodburners
Alaska Co., Inc.
480 West 5th Street
Bloomburg, Pennsylvania 17815

American Stovalator Fireplace Insert
East Manchester Road
Manchester Center, Vermont 05255

Ashley Heater Company
1604 17th Avenue, S.W.
Sheffield, Alabama 35660

Bell Foundry Company
5310 Southern Avenue
South Gate, California 90280

Better 'N Ben's
Hayes Equipment Corp.
150 New Britain Avenue
Unionville, Connecticut 06085

Cherokee Heating Systems, Inc.
P.O. Box 19356
Greensboro, North Carolina 27410

Cumberland Valley Metals, Inc.
P.O. Box 15666
Nashville, Tennessee 37215

Elco Fireplace
Petersen's Wood Heat Center, Inc.
P.O. Box 1, 309 Route 9
Lanoka Harbor, New Jersey 08734

Elite Fireplace Insert
Heathdelle Sales Associates, Inc.
Route 3
Meredith, New Hampshire 03253

Encon Ceiling Fan
(see Better 'N Ben's)

Esse Dragon
Windrose Corp.
59 River Road
Cos Cob, Connecticut 06807

EZ Set Energizer
(see Superior Fireplace Company)

Fire Rite Stoves
654 North Colony Street
Wallingford, Connecticut 06492

Forester Fireplace
(see United Stove Company)

The Free Heat Machine
Aquappliances, Inc.
135 Sunshine Lane
San Marcos, California 92069

Frontier
Jackson Frontier Co., Inc.
4065 West 11th Avenue
Eugene, Oregon 97402

Garrison Stove Works, Inc.
Box 412 Airport Road
Claremont, New Hampshire 03743

Hearth-Aid
Thermalite Corp.
P.O. Box 658
Brentwood, Tennessee 37027

Hearth-Mate
P.O. Box 766
C & D Distributors, Inc.
Old Saybrook, Connecticut 06475

Heat-A-Thon Circulator
Fireplace Grate Inc.
256 South Pine Street
Burlington, Wisconsin 53105

Heatform Circulating Fireplace
(see Superior Fireplace Company)

The Hot One
Energy Savers Co.
P.O. Box 111
Salem, Illinois 62881

Hydrohearth
Hydroheat, Inc.
P.O. Box 382
Ridgway, Pennsylvania 15853

177

The Insider
National Stove Works
Howe Cavern Road
Cobleskill, New York 12043

La Font Corp.
1319 Town Street
Prentice, Wisconsin 54556

Leyden Energy Conservation Corporation
Brattleboro Road
Leyden, Massachusetts 01337

Mohawk Industries, Inc.
P.O. Box 71
Adams, Massachusetts 01220

Moravian Fireplace Insert
Quaker Stove Company
200 West Fifth Street
Lansdale, Pennsylvania 19446

Morton Metalcraft
Route 98
Morton, Illinois 61550

Old Mill Fireplace Insert
DeVault Fab-Weld Company
Spring Mill Road
DeVault, Pennsylvania 19432

Ol' Hickory Woodstoves
P.O. Box 8008 Station A
Greenville, South Carolina 29604

Phoenix America Corp.
Suite 213 Executive Park
P.O. Box 1144
Asheville, North Carolina 28802

Pine Barren Stove, Inc.
Box 496, State Highway Route 72
Chatsworth, New Jersey 08019

Preway, Inc.
1430 Second Street North
Wisconsin Rapids, Wisconsin 54494

Pro-Former Engineering Corp.
8 Mear Road
Holbrook, Maine 02343

Retro-Fire
Contemporary Stove Works, Inc.
720 Oliver Drive
Suite L
Davis, California 95616

Russo Wood Stove Manufacturing Corp.
Water Street
Holbrook, Massachusetts 02343

Scandia
Franklin Cast Products, Inc.
1800 Post Road
Warwick, Rhode Island 02886

Sierra Marketing, Inc.
P.O. Box 346
Harrisonburg, Virginia 22801

Superior Fireplace Company
4325 Artesia Avenue
Fullerton, California 92633

Tamrak Industries
4000 Commerce Avenue
Fairfield, Alabama 35064

Temco, Inc.
4101 Charlotte Avenue
Nashville, Tennessee 37202

Tempview V
(see Mohawk Industries, Inc.)

Tempwood II
(see Mohawk Industries, Inc.)

Thermograte Enterprises, Inc.
P.O. Box 43021
2785 North Fairview Avenue
St. Paul, Minnesota 55164

Trident Heater Works
1600 Dowell Road
Giants Pass, Oregon 97526

United States Stove
South Pittsburg, Tennessee 37380

The Virginian Fireplace Insert
Wood Energy Marketing, Inc.
1932 Chapman Avenue
Roanoke, Virginia 24016

Wells Fireplace Furnace
Box 7079
Tucson, Arizona 85702

Weso Ceramic Tile Stove
Ceramic Radiant Heat
3699 Pleasant Drive
Lochmere, New Hampshire 03252